Getting into Primary Teaching

CRITICAL LEARNING

You might also like the following books from Critical Publishing

Teaching Systematic Synthetic Phonics and Early English
Jonathan Glazzard and Jane Stokoe
978-1-909330-09-2 In print

Primary School Placements: A Critical Guide to Outstanding Teaching
Catriona Robinson, Branwen Bingle and Colin Howard
978-1-909330-45-0 In print

Teaching and Learning Early Years Mathematics: Subject and Pedagogic Knowledge
Mary Briggs
978-1-909330-37-5 In print

Beyond Early Reading
Ed David Waugh and Sally Neaum
978-1-909330-41-2 In print

Inclusive Primary Teaching
Janet Goepel, Helen Childerhouse and Sheila Sharpe
978-1-909330-29-0 In print

Most of our titles are also available in a range of electronic formats. To order please go to our website www.criticalpublishing.com or contact our distributor, NBN International, 10 Thornbury Road, Plymouth PL6 7PP, telephone 01752 202301 or e-mail orders@ nbninternational.com.

Getting into Primary Teaching

Edited by David Owen & Cathy Burnett
Series Editor Andrew J Hobson

**CRITICAL
LEARNING**

First published in 2014 by Critical Publishing Ltd

British Library Cataloguing in Publication Data
A CIP record for this book is available from the British Library

ISBN: 978-1-909682-25-2

This book is also available in the following e-book formats:

Kindle ISBN: 978-1-909682-26-9
EPUB ISBN: 978-1-909682-27-6
Adobe e-book ISBN: 978-1-909682-28-3

Cover and text design by Greensplash Limited
Project Management by Out of House Publishing
Printed and bound in Great Britain by Bell and Bain, Glasgow

Critical Publishing
152 Chester Road
Northwich
CW8 4AL
www.criticalpublishing.com

FSC
www.fsc.org

MIX
Paper from
responsible sources
FSC® C007785

Contents

Meet the editors

David Owen taught in primary, secondary and residential environmental education settings before working at Sheffield Hallam University (SHU) as a teacher educator. He led the primary and early years programme at SHU for seven years before taking up the role of Head of the Department of Teacher Education. His research has focused on geographical education, e-learning and teacher education course development. He has worked closely with the Geographical Association and on a range of teacher education projects and was, until recently, a member of the editorial team for the *Primary Geographer* journal.

Cathy Burnett worked as an actor-teacher, primary teacher and literacy consultant before working in initial teacher education. She has been involved in supporting the initial and continuing development of teachers for many years. She has published a wide range of book chapters and journal articles with a focus on literacy education, new technologies and becoming a teacher. She is particularly interested in investigating classroom practices and in understanding the connections between learning in and out of school. She is currently co-editor of the United Kingdom Literacy Association journal, *Literacy*.

Andrew J Hobson is Professor of Education and Head of Education Research at the University of Brighton. He has previously been a teacher and mentor to newly qualified teachers. His research is concerned with the professional learning and development of beginners and more experienced teachers. He is editor of the *International Journal of Mentoring and Coaching in Education*.

Meet the authors

All of the contributing authors work at Sheffield Hallam University (SHU) in the Department of Teacher Education.

Jane Bartholomew is a senior lecturer in education. She is a trainee support tutor for the early years and primary courses and also leads a third year module. This focuses on developing trainees' confidence in the selection of planning approaches and reflects her interest in enquiry and learning skills. She is particularly interested in how teachers can promote effective learners through focusing on attitudes and cross-curricular skills.

Naomi Cooper is a senior lecturer on the primary BA and PGCE courses. She teaches on a variety of primary education modules and leads on English as an Additional Language and RE. As year leader for the third year of the BA course she liaises with students, staff and outside agencies in a number of different areas. Her research at Master's level related to inclusion of marginalised groups, including those with Special Educational Needs.

Karen Daniels is a senior lecturer in English. Her main duties are teaching on both undergraduate and postgraduate English modules with a focus on language and literacy in Key Stage 1 and the Early Years Foundation Stage. She is currently the subject leader for English.

Adrian Fearn is a principal lecturer in primary and early years education. He teaches mathematics and professional studies modules on all the BA and PGCE courses. As a university link tutor, he works in partnership with schools in the Sheffield region to support trainees' professional development while on school placements.

Janet Goepel was a teacher for many years and developed an interest in Special Educational Needs through having children with additional needs in her classes. She has taught children with profound and multiple learning difficulties who otherwise would have had to attend a special school, as well as those with dyslexia, dyspraxia, Attention Deficit Hyperactivity Disorder (ADHD) and social difficulties. She is now a senior lecturer teaching inclusion at SHU and hopes to pass on her passion for inclusive practice to trainee teachers.

Julia Myers is a principal lecturer and primary and early years staff group lead. She joined the English team at SHU in 2000 and became English subject leader from 2009 to 2011. For several years she has been involved in a variety of LTA (Learning, Teaching and Assessment) projects, including the development of feedback on students' academic work, and since 2011 has been the lead for LTA within the Department of Teacher Education.

Sarah Williams is a senior lecturer and Year 2 course leader on the BA primary and early years teacher education course, and is a primary physical education specialist. She has spent the last ten years working with primary and secondary schools in Sheffield developing opportunities within physical education and school sport. She currently teaches undergraduate and postgraduate trainees and supports a number of professional development programmes for teachers.

Series editor's introduction

This book provides you with an expert, comprehensive and up-to-date account of the process of getting into primary school teaching. It will be a particularly invaluable source of guidance for those of you who are about to embark upon the process of becoming a teacher, or who are considering doing so. Such a decision must not be taken lightly, and it is essential that you are prepared for what lies ahead. The experience of learning to teach – whether in primary, secondary or further education – is, like teaching itself, extremely challenging and invariably involves both *delightful highs and distressing lows* (Bullough, 2009, p 34), associated with feelings of enjoyment, excitement, hope, satisfaction and reward on the one hand, and vulnerability, fear, frustration, humiliation and despair on the other (Bullough, 2009; Hobson et al, 2009)! The process of becoming a *primary* school teacher, and doing so in the second decade of the twenty-first century – whether in England or further afield – poses its particular challenges.

Such challenges, and means of meeting and overcoming them, are a major focus of this text, and are very familiar to its editors and chapter authors. Among them, these writers boast decades of experience of working as primary teachers and leaders, of preparing (supporting, educating and training) new primary teachers, and of supporting the professional learning and development of more experienced teachers of primary school children. They are expert practitioners and teacher educators, subject specialists, and include nationally and internationally renowned researchers in their respective fields.

As well as their own considerable knowledge and experience, the authors also draw on the latest research and on the recent experiences and 'voices' of primary school pupils, teachers, head teachers and student teachers to help explain key aspects of learning to become – and being – a primary school teacher. This, together with the use of real-life examples and the reflective tasks provided, makes *Getting into Primary Teaching* an interesting, informative and enjoyable read.

In keeping with the underlying principles of its publisher, *Getting into Primary Teaching* urges readers to develop (or develop further) an informed *critical* approach to teaching, learning, education and their own professional development. This is important because your development as a critically reflective practitioner will enable you to continue to learn – both from experience and other sources – in order to become and then remain a good or excellent teacher. It is important to recognise that this will not happen overnight. Teaching is much more than learning and 'delivering' a body of knowledge, and becoming an excellent teacher requires much more than being apprenticed to, in order to learn from, an existing excellent teacher. Among other things, it also requires:

- o *understanding* – for example, of how pupils learn, of how different pupils learn in different ways, of various barriers to learning which different pupils experience to different degrees, and of means of potentially overcoming such barriers;

- the discovery and development of a *teacher identity*;

- the discovery and development of your *personal and unique* approach(es) to teaching and facilitating learning;

- continual *evaluation* and *adaptation* of such approaches for different learners in different contexts; and

- the development of *resilience* and mental strength, to enable you to 'bounce back' from the inevitable lows associated with becoming and being a teacher, and to cope with frequent changes to the curriculum and with the intense degree of scrutiny to which teachers' work is currently subject in England and some other educational systems, which Pat Mahony and colleagues have (rightly in my view) termed *surveillance overkill* (Mahony et al, 2004, p 440).

Getting into Primary Teaching addresses all of these important matters, while providing invaluable insights into a range of other key concerns pertinent to becoming a primary school teacher, including:

- what it is like to be a primary teacher and what it means to be a professional;

- how to successfully apply for a place on different types of initial teacher preparation programmes (commonly but simplistically termed 'teacher training');

- the teaching of English and mathematics;

- meeting the needs of all learners (Special Educational Needs and inclusion);

- planning and implementing a creative curriculum; and

- placing learning at the centre of your journey towards becoming a qualified teacher.

I trust that you will learn much from the following chapters, and that they in turn will help you to learn much from your subsequent experience of becoming a teacher, should you choose to embark upon this potentially treacherous yet exciting and hugely rewarding career choice.

Andrew J Hobson, 2014

REFERENCES

Bullough, RV, Jr. (2009) Seeking Eudaimonia: The Emotions in Learning to Teach and to Mentor, in Schutz, P and Zembylas, M (eds) *Teacher Emotion Research: The Impact on Teachers' Lives*. New York: Springer, pp 33–53.

Hobson, AJ, Malderez, A and Tracey, L (2009) *Navigating Initial Teacher Training: Becoming a Teacher*. London and New York: Routledge.

Mahony, P, Menter, I and Hextall, I (2004) The Emotional Impact of Performance-Related Pay on Teachers in England. *British Educational Research Journal*, 30(3): 435–56.

Acknowledgements

We would like to thank all the teachers, student-teachers, head-teachers and children who kindly shared their perspectives on teaching and provided examples of inspirational practice. We would also like to thank Andy Hobson and Julia Morris at Critical Publishing for their helpful feedback.

Thanks also to the following for their kind permission to use copyright material in this book.

Figure 6.3, page 102, Making connections diagram reproduced by kind permission of Anne Cockburn and Derek Haylock.

Figure 7.1, page 118, Hierarchical method for cross-curricular development diagram reproduced by kind permission of Jonathan Barnes.

Figure 7.2, page 125, TASC wheel reproduced by kind permission of Belle Wallace.

Every effort has been made to trace copyright holders and to obtain their permission for the use of copyright material. The Publisher and authors will gladly receive information enabling them to rectify any error or omission in subsequent editions.

1 Introduction

David Owen

This book will support your application to be a primary school teacher and will help you develop the knowledge, skills and understanding to gain preparatory experience in a school and become a successful teacher. The authors of each chapter have all been successful primary teachers and have worked with many student teachers in initial teacher education, as well as supporting the continuing professional development of more experienced teachers. It is worth noting that, while much of the advice contained in this book will be relevant to those interested in teaching in various contexts, sections on policy and curriculum frameworks focus primarily on England. On occasion we do invite you to consider alternative frameworks in Wales, Scotland and Northern Ireland.

STRUCTURE AND CONTENT OF THE BOOK

Each chapter of the book has the following learning features to help you engage with the topics that are explored.

○ **Reflective tasks**: these are activities, questions and stimuli for thinking about teaching. They will help you actively engage with the research extracts, case studies and examples from schools that are provided.

○ **Pupil/teacher/student voice**: these case studies give you the opportunity to hear directly from pupils, student teachers and qualified teachers. You will have the opportunity to talk with such people on school placements during your initial teacher preparation programme, but this feature collects a wider range of views than can be found in a single school or small number of schools. These scenarios and classroom examples are also the basis for many of the reflective tasks.

○ **Research focus**: here you are introduced to important research projects that have helped shape primary education.

○ **Jargon busters**: do you know your NCTL from your NASBTT? Your summative from your formative assessment? Primary education is full of jargon and acronyms, and this feature explains and demystifies phrases you may hear in a school or read in a primary school curriculum textbook. Words highlighted are included in jargon buster sections at the end of each chapter.

○ **Taking it further**: want to find out more about the issues discussed in each chapter? Follow up the accessible web-links and books explained in this section.

○ **Progress checklist**: use this list to systematically prepare for an application for a primary course. Each chapter will give you the opportunity to audit your understanding and develop your knowledge.

In Chapter 2, Cathy Burnett draws on teachers' stories to explore the nature of teaching in the twenty-first century. She highlights the varied roles that teachers are expected to fulfil and the rewards, opportunities and challenges associated with these. Cathy introduces the idea of 'professionalism' and explores how teachers work alongside others, including parents/carers and other members of the local community, and colleagues in schools and in multi-agency teams. She describes the different contexts in which teachers work and introduces the range of career opportunities available to those with Qualified Teacher Status (QTS). You are encouraged to reflect on the skills, knowledge and experience you might bring to teaching and to consider how values and beliefs are significant to how teachers teach and the kinds of experiences they provide.

In Chapter 3, David Owen provides practical guidance on making an application for an initial teacher preparation programme. While recognising that recruitment requirements and procedures vary between routes and institutions, he outlines key elements of the applications process: learning from school experience; writing a personal statement; evidencing subject knowledge in English and mathematics; preparation for, and taking, the skills tests; resilience and professionalism; understanding the application process; and success in individual and group interviews. The chapter provides guidance on writing applications and preparing for interviews, and draws on personal accounts by admissions tutors and head teachers.

Chapter 4 (also written by David Owen) explores how you learn to become a teacher. It introduces the National Curriculum in England (DfE, 2013) and gives details of the curriculum arrangements in Wales, Scotland and Northern Ireland. Teaching is a commonplace activity but can be difficult to explain, so the chapter reviews beliefs about teaching and how these beliefs influence types of teacher preparation programmes. It introduces the concept of the reflective practitioner and reviews approaches to reflection you can use as an adult learner. A common thread within any teacher preparation programme is the need to meet the Teachers' Standards (DfE, 2012) and these are reviewed and explained alongside the roles of school-based mentors and host class teachers.

In Chapter 5, Karen Daniels and Julia Myers explore the nature of subject knowledge in English and how this is relevant to your teaching. They begin by explaining the nature and centrality of language and literacy in daily life and present examples of children's use of literacy in their lives beyond the classroom. They then examine the changing nature of literacy and the impact of digital technologies on our understanding of what is meant by reading, writing and texts. Karen and Julia present an overview of aspects of children's development in speaking and listening, reading and writing over the primary years. They describe current approaches to the teaching of English and illustrate these with examples of classroom practice and commentary from experienced classroom practitioners. The role of children's literature and approaches to teaching early reading, including phonics, are also considered. The chapter highlights the knowledge required to plan, teach and assess children in English. It provides guidance to help you review and develop your subject knowledge prior to beginning or applying for a teacher preparation programme. Karen and Julia highlight the knowledge that all users of English bring to the subject and identify ways in which you can build upon and extend this through further reading, resources and activities.

In Chapter 6 Adrian Fearn introduces primary school mathematics and approaches to teaching and learning this subject. He highlights how important it is for teachers to be confident about mathematics and to have a positive attitude to mathematical learning. The chapter provides you with reflective tasks to clarify your own views on mathematics and learning. Adrian provides examples to explain the classroom teaching of mathematics, describes current approaches and illustrates these with examples of classroom practice and practical mathematical challenges. The final part of the chapter provides the opportunity for you to begin building subject knowledge related to children's misconceptions in mathematical reasoning.

In Chapter 7 Sarah Williams explores how schools develop curricula that are suited to the needs of their pupils. She examines creativity across the curriculum through exploring approaches to teaching and learning designed to engage and inspire learners. She focuses on the key concepts behind designing a creative curriculum. Sarah explores how a creative curriculum is defined, through reviewing practice and theory around engagement, enquiry and experiential learning. She provides case studies of creative teaching, which show how successful teachers develop and sustain an inspiring learning environment in their classrooms. Sarah invites you to consider the ownership of knowledge and the learning process, exploring the social context and the role of classroom talk, and the significance of motivation and flexibility in learning situations.

Next, in Chapter 8, Jane Bartholomew explores involving children in their development as learners through 'learning to learn'. This chapter considers what is understood by 'learning to learn' and encourages you to reflect on your own experience of and attitudes to learning. Drawing on case studies of classroom practice, the chapter explores how teachers can enable children to become effective learners across the curriculum and beyond, through: making explicit learning objectives and/or learning outcomes; focusing on skills and attitudes; developing pupil autonomy; and establishing communities of learning. Jane invites critical appraisal of some widely used initiatives, such as 'visual, auditory and kinaesthetic learning (VAK)' and 'brain-based learning'. The chapter explores the role of assessment for learning and behaviour for learning. Throughout the chapter, Jane considers a range of practical approaches and contexts for learning.

Chapter 9 introduces the concept of inclusion, with several scenarios from practice to enable you to identify with the theme. Here Janet Goepel and Naomi Cooper introduce key vocabulary, such as barriers to learning, Special Educational Needs and Disability (SEND) and English as an Additional Language (EAL). The chapter also explores barriers to learning which are present in some primary classrooms. Janet and Naomi provide case studies of inclusive classrooms and inclusive curricula, through which they outline some of the benefits to all learners of inclusive environments (with a focus on children with SEN and children with EAL). Quotes and examples from children, parents and teachers help you to think about issues from different points of view. Finally, the authors provide questions to frame your thinking when you are visiting schools or engaged in practical experience.

The Conclusion summarises the key themes discussed in the book and outlines how preparing to become a primary teacher may change in the future. David Owen reviews the employment prospects (at the time of writing) for those training to be a teacher. He also considers how, after gaining a place on a teacher preparation programme, successful candidates can subsequently enhance their employment prospects.

REFERENCES

Department for Education (DfE) (2012) *Teachers' Standards*. London: Crown
   Publications. Available at www.gov.uk/government/publications/teachers-standards.

Department for Education (DfE) (2013) *The National Curriculum in England: Framework
   Document for Consultation*. London: Crown Publications. Available at www.media.
   education.gov.uk/assets/files/pdf/n/national%20curriculum%20consultation%20
   -%20framework%20document.pdf.

Why teach?

Cathy Burnett

INTRODUCTION

Being a primary teacher can be rewarding, exhilarating, intellectually stimulating, creative and good fun. It can also be frustrating, difficult and exhausting. This chapter explores what is involved in being a teacher, highlighting the rewards and challenges of this very complex role. It provides an overview of what you will teach and other aspects of a teacher's responsibilities. It explores what it means to be a 'professional' and emphasises the importance of working with others. At various points you will hear from five teachers at different stages of their career – Natasha Morris, Mark Bennett, Skander Hussain, Hilary Malden and Kate Cosgrove – who reflect on their own experiences of 'getting into teaching'. The chapter ends by outlining a series of possible career routes open to teachers.

There are many reasons why you may be considering becoming a primary teacher. You may have a deep commitment to supporting children's learning and want to make a difference to children's lives. You may have spent time in classrooms, perhaps as a teaching assistant or volunteer, and believe you have the qualities a teacher needs. You may really enjoy working with children, having gained experience through supporting after-school clubs or sports activities. Alternatively, you may recognise that teaching offers the opportunity to develop skills associated with leadership and organisation that you can go on to use in another career. Or you may have a young family and feel that school holidays will mean you can spend more time with their children. It is likely that a number of these reasons, and others, have led you to think more about the possibility of being a teacher.

Teacher voice

Deciding to become a teacher

Mark: *I went to university because it was what my friends did, and initially studied sport, physical education and community studies with the intention of becoming a PE teacher. While at uni I volunteered for three years with an organisation that sent coaches into primary* schools to run after-school clubs and PE lessons. This inspired me to work with primary-aged children and at the end of my degree I applied for a primary PGCE, but was rejected because I did not have enough experience of working in schools. I applied for a job as a teaching assistant, to get that experience and to see if teaching was what I really wanted to do (and whether I was cut out for it). The year I had as a teaching assistant really set me up for teaching. It made me realise I wanted to teach and also gave me the building blocks to hit the ground running when I started my PGCE, particularly in managing behaviour in classrooms.

Hilary: I've been teaching for about 30 years, with a break in the middle when I had my children. My mum was a teacher so that's why I think I thought of going into teaching. After school I did a psychology degree and then a PGCE. After ten years I did an MA and trained to be an educational psychologist but after working as an educational psychologist for a year, I went back to teaching as I decided I'd rather be in the classroom. I missed the relationships with the children and the creative side. I work part-time – three days a week. I went part-time after I had my children and have stayed part-time since then.

Skander: I always knew I wanted to be in a caring role as I had always looked after members of my family, but I didn't know exactly what route that would take. At 16 I completed a two-week placement at my former primary school and I fell in love with the whole experience. The school had changed a great deal since I was there. I thought maybe I too could achieve and be part of a change. I was also spurred on by being told I would not succeed by teachers who taught me. When I got the points I needed for university I felt really good about my achievement and I thought how good it would feel to help children to achieve what I was feeling. I came from an economically deprived area and I felt I'd disproved what people had said about what I could achieve. I was also really encouraged by my family, who wanted us to aspire to do the best we could.

Natasha: When I was doing my GCSEs I wasn't very motivated. I knew I could get by with the bare minimum and devoted most of my energy to the acting I was doing out of school. I didn't apply for uni when I left school because I felt despondent about school. During the following year I remembered that when I was younger I'd wanted to be a primary teacher as I'd really enjoyed primary school. So I took a gap year, working at the post office and spending half a day a week in a primary school. The decision to be a primary teacher was partly about childhood memories and partly about a desire to provide a good experience for children. I also thought it was a career where I would always learn and that school would be a place where I could apply all the drama I'd done and use creative approaches.

Kate: My first degree was architecture, though I didn't go on to practise as an architect. I found a job in a related field that lasted a few years and then the first recession hit the UK and I found myself out of work. I worked as a musician for a while, but then I decided to leave work to raise my children. I had always had at the back of my mind that I would like to teach, but I didn't really know what. My mum was a teacher and to be honest, it seemed like the family legacy, so I went to a few schools to find out what it was like and if I really wanted to follow in my mum's footsteps. I got a place on a PGCE. When I started I was a mature student and many others on the course were too, mostly mums returning to work after raising their children. The rest of the students were straight from a degree course, so we were a mixed bunch. When I started teaching, my subject specialism was mathematics. But in my first job the maths co-ordinator was very well established and the role of literacy co-ordinator came up... It kind of fell to me, and I have been literacy co-ordinator ever since, in every school I have worked in.

Reflective task

- Which different experiences and motivations led these teachers into teaching?

- What experiences were valuable to them in helping them decide to be teachers?

- Which barriers did they have to overcome?

WHAT'S INVOLVED IN TEACHING?

Being professional

Teaching is often referred to as a profession and considering what this means is an important part of becoming a teacher. Being a professional concerns how you relate to others and behave as a teacher. In everyday life we often refer to people as 'behaving professionally' and by this we tend to mean that they are conducting themselves in a way that is sensitive to our needs. This might mean being polite and efficient, but also making sure that everyone is treated fairly or equitably. 'Behaving professionally' is certainly an important part of being a teacher. However, many would suggest that 'being a professional' involves more than this.

Opinions about what 'being a professional' involves vary but it may be seen as including some or all of the following (Goepel, 2012):

o having the specialist knowledge needed to respond flexibly to different situations (for example, meeting the needs of particular learners, working with colleagues to decide how to respond to policy initiatives, deciding how best to work with other partners to support children's learning);

o continuing to learn through professional development activities;

o standing up for the interests of the children you work with while being open to new perspectives and possibilities;

o becoming part of a teaching community through working with others (in your own school or from other schools);

o acting within statutory frameworks, eg, linked to pay and conditions.

Research focus

Evans, L (2011) The 'Shape' of Teacher Professionalism in England: Professional Standards, Performance Management, Professional Development and the Changes Proposed in the 2010 White Paper. *British Educational Research Journal*, 37(5): 851–70.

Linda Evans describes three components of professionalism including:

1. a behavioural component (what teachers do and achieve while at work);

2. an attitudinal component (teachers' perceptions, beliefs and views); and

3. an intellectual component (teachers' knowledge, understanding and ability to analyse what they do).

Reflective task

During your initial teacher preparation, you will be asked to satisfy certain professional standards and exhibit professional values. Look at the standards for teachers in England and compare them with those for teachers in Scotland, Northern Ireland and Wales. You can easily find these by searching the internet.

o Does each set of standards address all three of the components identified by Evans?

o How are expectations from each country similar? Or different?

o Which aspects of professionalism do they seem to prioritise?

o Consider possible reasons for any differences.

Teacher voice

The scope of teaching

New entrants to the teaching profession are often surprised by the range and scope of what is involved. Natasha, Skander, Hilary and Mark describe how they see teaching.

Natasha: *There were lots of aspects of teaching that I wasn't aware of. It's not just about 'delivery' but all kinds of other things such as being a subject leader, managing a budget, writing reports for governors, communicating with parents and liaising with other agencies. You have to develop a huge range of skills very quickly. I was also surprised at how much I didn't know in terms of subject knowledge, and the depth of knowledge that was needed in English, science, maths and ICT in order to teach those subjects. In order to teach well I have to do so much research.*

Skander: *As a teacher you never stop learning. You become self-critical as you want the best for the children. Also, teaching constantly changes. It's changed so much in just the short period that I've been teaching. You're constantly reinventing and changing yourself. I'm not shy. I've always demanded attention and I used these traits when I became a teacher. I also used my culture, my ethnicity and my personality in my teaching. Now I'm more of a facilitator than a deliverer of children's learning, allowing them to develop cognitively but also supporting their holistic development, their social development into the people they're going to be.*

Hilary: *There are more and more pressures now, and expectations seem to be getting higher and higher in terms of what children achieve, and you have to be more and more accountable, which means spending time gathering data rather than on teaching and learning. One of our student teachers commented, 'Everybody here does everything so fast.' People don't realise the speed at which teachers work and how intensive it is. One minute you're talking to a child about maths, the next you're talking to a parent, and then it's something else.*

Mark: *Teaching must be one of the biggest balancing acts around when it comes to managing everything you have to do. I would say teaching*

> *involves being very organised, mentally strong and empathetic. A teacher is constantly problem-solving, putting themselves in a child's place, thinking about ways of putting something across to a class or individuals. At the same time, teachers need energy, especially near the end of an eight-week half-term!*

Reflective task

○ Having read these teachers' thoughts, and reflected on your own prior experience of teachers, teaching and schools, make a list of the various roles you might expect a teacher to fulfil. Here are some to start with: administrator, assessor, carer, director, enabler, evaluator, explainer, facilitator, guide, instructor, leader, manager, mentor, organiser, performer, researcher.

○ You may wish to present this list of terms to a teacher you know and ask them to talk through how they feel each relates to what they do as part of their role.

○ Consider each in terms of your current skills and experiences to date (from paid or voluntary work, hobbies and relationships as well as classroom experience). Sort them into three groups:

   1. those with which you are already confident;

   2. those with which you are currently gaining experience; and

   3. those you are concerned about.

○ Reflect on the skills and experiences you will bring to initial teacher preparation, and those you need to develop before or when you begin your initial teacher education programme.

WHAT WILL YOU TEACH?

The vast majority of primary teachers are generalists who teach their class all the subjects in the curriculum. You will find details of these subjects in Chapter 4. Many schools develop learning across the curriculum, integrating learning from different subjects through activities and experiences (this is explored in more depth in Chapter 7). This means that if you have a real passion for a particular subject you may prefer to train as a secondary teacher. If, however, you decide on a career as a primary teacher you may still have opportunities to build on your interest, passion or expertise linked to a particular subject. Sometimes primary schools have specialist teachers that take all children for certain subjects, eg, PE or music. You may become a subject leader or curriculum co-ordinator with responsibility for developing the curriculum and teaching approaches across the school in a particular subject. You may also run extra-curricular activities, such as after-school or lunchtime clubs, or booster sessions for children working towards national assessments. There are also reasons why you may teach children from other classes at certain times of the week. For example, the school may organise children into ability groups for certain subjects, eg, mathematics and English/literacy, so that teachers take a mixed ability group from different classes for these subjects.

But it is not just about which subjects you will teach. Contrary to popular belief, working as a primary teacher involves far more than 'delivering' a set of skills or knowledge to children. When children enter the class, they are not 'blank slates' or 'empty vessels', but bring with them a multitude of experiences, enthusiasms and understandings. When you visit schools, take time to find out about children's interests and be alert to the different languages children speak and the social and cultural experiences they bring with them to school. Children need to know that their experiences are valued and as a teacher you will want to find ways of recognising and building on the skills and knowledge they bring.

As a teacher you will act 'in loco parentis'. You will be expected to take decisions that have each child's best interests at heart and always act to ensure children's health and welfare. This means thinking about practical things such as health and safety, but also caring for a child's emotional and social wellbeing. You may hear teachers referring to the *ethos* of a school. This refers to values and beliefs about what matters: for example, how to behave towards others, and what kind of learning is seen as worthwhile. Adults' behaviour is central to ethos: the way you treat children and respond to their interests (or not) lets children know what matters. The way you interact – with children and your colleagues – models what is expected in terms of collaboration, communication and mutual respect. Moreover, as explored further in Chapter 8, if adults present themselves as learners, children see that learning is an ongoing process. Teachers therefore need to *constantly reflect upon and question what they do* (Bath, 2009, p 3) and consider what messages children may take from how you behave and the kinds of learning opportunities you provide.

Reflective task

When you are in school, reflect on what each of the following suggest about what is seen to be important in terms of: the nature of learning; what children are learning; and relationships.

- Verbal and non-verbal interaction (eg, who is allowed to talk, when and for what purposes).
- Resources (eg, whose cultural and social experiences are represented in the resources children can access, such as books and computer programs).
- Classroom environments (eg, displays, arrangement of furniture).
- Feedback (written or oral feedback on what children do in class).
- The curriculum (what children are learning).
- Involvement of other adults (such as parents/carers, teaching assistants).

TEACHING AS TEAMWORK

Working with others is a key part of the teacher's role and you will need to develop the interpersonal skills to do this. You will be expected to work with colleagues to plan and assess children's learning and to develop school policies and approaches. A priority will be to develop good relationships with parents so you can work together as partners to support children's learning. This includes keeping parents informed about children's learning and social and emotional welfare at school, as well as providing support for parents to support children's learning at home. However, this should not just be *one-way traffic* (Marsh, 2003) but involve ongoing dialogue with parents and carers. This means listening to parents' concerns and learning from them about their child's interests and experiences. As a teacher you will need to think carefully about:

o   how you communicate with parents about children's progress;

o   planning and supporting home learning;

o   making decisions about what happens in school;

o   collaborating with and learning from the local community.

Many people enter the teaching profession after having spent time as a teaching assistant. If this applies to you, you will be able to draw on your experience of working with teachers to support children's learning. What helped you do this? What kind of skills did you need and how were you supported? How (and how often) did you liaise with the teacher? You will also be aware that many different adults may support the learning of children in one class or contribute to the support in different ways. If you do not have experience of working as a teaching assistant, you may be surprised at the number of people who work with the teacher to support learning. These may include those based at school such as:

o   learning support assistants;

o   bilingual and multilingual support assistants or teachers;

o   the school's Special Educational Needs Co-ordinator (SENCO);

o   governors.

It also includes those who work with a number of schools such as:

o   educational psychologists;

o   the traveller education service;

o   ethnic minority and traveller achievement grant (EMTAG) teachers;

o   ch and language therapists;

ists.

hose working with and for the child will (or should) be aiming to support pendent learning. This does not mean just helping them to complete tasks but helping them to develop the skills and understandings that will ultimately enable them to learn for themselves. Sometimes, when children work closely with another adult for much of the day they can miss out on opportunities to work with other children. Consequently you may see a learning support assistant working with a group of children (to facilitate their learning as they work together) or supporting the child to use or develop independent learning skills.

Multi-agency working

In recent years there has been an expectation that schools will work closely with other agencies (such as social workers, health professionals or support workers) and parents to make sure that support for children seen as vulnerable is co-ordinated effectively and that information is shared between different parties. This is challenging as different professional groups and agencies tend to see things from different points of view and use different language to refer to children's needs and the kind of support required. This is essentially because they bring different expertise and ways of understanding and responding to a child's needs. Working with others then means listening to and learning from other agencies but also ensuring that other agencies are able to see the child's needs from your perspective as a teacher (Frost, 2005). You will need to work as an advocate for the children and parents/carers you work with, representing their interests and ensuring others understand their perspectives and experiences. This means having an open mind, listening carefully and being sensitive to what is important to them and the extent to which the school and other agencies are meeting their needs.

WHERE MIGHT YOU TEACH?

There are many different kinds of primary school. Schools vary in location, for example they may be in rural, urban, suburban or inner-city areas. They also vary in demographic make-up, for example, some schools will attract children who speak many different languages. Schools vary in size too and this will have implications for age range in each class and for class sizes. Very small schools are likely to have mixed age classes, while larger ones will have what is referred to as two or three form entry (ie, two or three parallel classes in each year group). Most primary schools offer education across the primary age but you will find some separate infant and junior schools (for 5–7-year-olds and 7–11-year-olds respectively). In some areas, you may find first and middle schools (usually for 5–9-year-olds and 9–13-year-olds). Some schools will offer early years or pre-school provision whilst others will not. Schools will also be governed in different ways. Some will be faith schools. In England, you will also find academies, or teaching schools, which operate as part of teaching school alliances. In 2011 free schools were introduced in England. Academies, free schools and private schools do not have to follow the national curriculum, so you are likely to encounter different kinds of specialisms or approaches if you are placed in one of these schools. Schools also vary according to the principles and values that inform what they do. They are led and managed in different ways and this has implications for staff relationships, the curriculum, ethos and resources.

Teacher voice

Working in different schools

Hilary: I've been at my current school for 13 years. The school is quite small with just one class per year group. The school has a very diverse community, which I like, and there is lots of contact with parents and the community. The school's been awarded a Gold Artsmark for its emphasis on art and gained an Investors in Diversity award for its community work and its curriculum, which takes account of the diversity of the children and provides global perspectives. As it's a small school, you have to take on a lot of roles. I'm a member of the senior leadership team and also co-ordinate art, music and mentorship for student teachers.

Mark: The current school I work in is a one-and-a-half form entry school. The school attracts children from a local council estate and a more affluent area a short distance from the school. The school, as a result of a longstanding head and long-established staff base, has very much a family feel and I really do feel it's at the centre of the community.

Kate: My school has around 300 children from Reception to Year 6. It's a great place to work. We are like a team and look after each other. The staff is a strong team of practitioners who enjoy research and study, with a culture of staff development. We do a lot of work using Web 2.0 tools such as blogging and Twitter, which engages parents and the community in school life by bringing the classrooms to life on the internet. This has had a big impact on home–school communication, and has enriched the children's learning by allowing them to share so many of their experiences with their parents.

Skander: My first job was in a primary school. In my third year I moved to a school for children with profound and multiple learning difficulties where I teach a primary class. I work with nine children and teaching assistants and am numeracy co-ordinator for the school.

Having reflected on the range of schools you will encounter, it is worth noting that you are likely to see many changes in schools during your career. For example, new technologies offer opportunities for children to share knowledge and ideas and collaborate with people in other locations. In the future, this may mean that schools look very different from the way they do today.

Reflective task

Gain an overview of different kinds of schools by browsing school websites from your local area or further afield. Think about what type of school you are attracted to. Consider:

○   what each school seems to feel is important;

○   the values that are (or appear to be) promoted;

○   what you can learn about the curriculum and other activities in which the school is involved.

THE REWARDS AND CHALLENGES OF TEACHING

Many of those who enter teaching do so because they want to make a difference to children's lives, and most people who stay in teaching do so because of their commitment to children's learning (Day and Saunders, 2006). Teachers may be fascinated by the learning process and committed to finding creative, motivating ways to support children's development. They may also care deeply about children's emotional and social wellbeing. They may have other commitments, linked to issues of equality for example, and want to work in education to empower children to take control of their lives.

Teacher voice

The rewards of teaching

Natasha: *The thing I really enjoy is 9am–3pm with the children. It's absolutely great being in the classroom. I particularly enjoy it when I'm doing something for the first time. I also enjoy it when the children are really excited and engaged. I enjoy it when they come to a conclusion and have changed their thinking or their awareness. I also like seeing children really proud about something – something that hasn't come easily but they have genuinely really achieved, in literacy or numeracy or behaviour – that means they feel better about themselves.*

Kate: *What I enjoy most about my job is working with the children. I am passionate about stories and books and storytelling and new technologies. I try to weave together all of my passions and expertise to give the children in my class the very best experiences* of a twenty-first-century classroom. One of the best parts for me is when children come into the classroom in the morning with work that they have done at home, encouraged by the things they have learned the day before. There's nothing better than being brought a poem first thing in the morning to brighten your day.

Hilary: I really like the variety – and the creative projects and all the extra things we do, like residential visits. You get to know the children very, very well and see their progress, see them growing up. That's very rewarding, particularly when you teach them for two years in a row, which happens sometimes. You also get to know the parents well and sometimes see the children you've taught bringing their own children to school.

Skander: The enjoyment you get from knowing you have made a difference in the life of the children is second to none. I love assessment. We use 'learning journeys' to show how the children have progressed. ['Learning journeys' are visual records of a child's achievement during a year.] At my school the children get dropped off and picked up in taxis so you don't see the parents as often as in a mainstream school. The learning journeys are wonderful as the parents can experience visually what the children have experienced that year.

Mark: I enjoy the sense of community you have within a school – the bond that is made by everyone belonging. For me, though, I most enjoy working with children and building relationships with them. Seeing the excitement when they enjoy something and watching them grow and change during the year they are in your class. There cannot be many jobs out there that compare to teaching when it comes to gaining a sense of achievement, making people happy and influencing people's lives on a major scale ... and the holidays are great!

As these comments suggest, teaching can be a highly rewarding career. Nevertheless, a significant number of teachers do leave the profession within five years and so it is important to have a realistic idea about teaching before you apply for initial teacher preparation. It seems that some people withdraw from teacher preparation because they have unrealistic expectations of what teaching involves. While it is difficult to collect evidence about reasons for withdrawal – as people may be reluctant to give their true reasons, a common reason given is the heavy workload involved, and those most likely to withdraw seem to be those who are less committed to teaching as a profession when they apply (Hobson et al, 2009). Teaching certainly is not an easy career option and it is important to be prepared for its challenges as well as its rewards.

Before embarking on a career in teaching you will want to explore arrangements for pay and conditions. Currently all teachers are entitled to a half day out of class each week for planning, marking and preparation. Guidelines have also been produced relating to what teachers should, and should not, be required to do. Nevertheless, the time needed to complete tasks associated with administration, planning, record-keeping, assessment, reporting and management, along with other extra-curricular commitments, mean that a teacher's day does not begin and end with the children's day, and time during school holidays is devoted to planning and preparation.

You also need to be aware that policies (based on national or school decisions) will influence what and how you teach. As explored above, set curricula are likely to outline what you must teach and you may be required to teach in a certain way. At some times you may see these policies as helpful frameworks. At others, you may disagree with priorities or approaches and feel that you have insufficient autonomy. Your work will also be evaluated: by the children you teach of course but also by colleagues, your head teacher and inspection teams. You will be aware that the media can be unkind to teachers and you will get used to hearing negative reports about what happens in schools – which many teachers feel misinterpret what actually happens. All this can be exhausting and teachers often feel unable to devote as much time as they would like to the things they feel are important. Moreover, teaching can be highly emotional (Hargreaves, 1998). Engaging with pupils with different interests and preoccupations is challenging, and when things do not go according to plan, it can sometimes feel like a very personal failure. All teachers find different aspects of their work difficult at times.

Teacher voice

The challenges of teaching

Natasha: *The things I like less include the paperwork. It's really time-consuming and not necessarily helpful, which is frustrating. It comes and goes, particularly with Ofsted. I also don't like the media construction of teachers and the public slating teachers get. This is really unhelpful particularly when you work really hard. I also don't like being tired – teaching is incredibly tiring.*

Kate: *It is a lot of work. Sometimes, the last thing you want to do in an evening is sit down and mark 60 books, and managing the workload can be difficult. But it's worth it.*

Skander: *Entering teaching, you need a good GP as in the first couple of years you catch everything. I ended up having my tonsils out in* *my second year of teaching. I also find it challenging to get the right balance between being professional and getting emotionally attached to the children. I lost one of my children and had to go to the funeral and it was devastating.*

Mark: *First of all, the hardest thing I found was not being able to be the best all the time. There was not the time or the energy to do this. Also ... pressure! As a teaching assistant and student-teacher, the buck never stopped with me. As a teacher I quickly realised that things were ultimately down to me. People were not just going to tell me what to do. I had to be more resourceful in my approach to dealing with problems.*

Hilary: *As a new teacher, you have to work with a lot of adults – parents, colleagues, support staff, other agencies, the local community. This can be quite daunting if you're young as you need to build good relationships with all these people. Every school is different and you have to be prepared to follow their policies even if you don't agree. So it's important to find one in which you're happy. There are also worries sometimes about safeguarding and the responsibility when you take children outside school.*

In recent years there has been a lot of interest in promoting teacher resilience. Most simply 'resilience' is the ability to keep going even when facing tough challenges and is associated with characteristics such as optimism, a sense of humour and the ability to handle stress (Tait, 2008). Our levels of resilience are likely to vary according to our circumstances and according to what we are being asked to do. The people and support systems available will also be significant. We could argue that it is the job of policy-makers and managers to ensure that workloads are reasonable and that effective support is provided for teachers (Price et al, 2012). However, teaching has always been demanding and complex and if you are considering entering the profession you will need to consider how you will deal with competing demands and tough challenges. It is worth noting that, in England, teacher education providers have been asked to judge candidates' resilience as part of the selection process for initial teacher preparation. So if you do apply, you may need to describe what is meant by resilience and the strategies you will use to deal with challenges.

Resilience, importantly, is something that you can develop. As you become more confident as a teacher your sense of resilience is likely to increase as you develop a range of ways to solve problems and become more confident in trialling approaches and taking risks. Most people need others to help them do this. This means that part of being resilient is about building strong relationships so you have people around you who can listen, help you reflect on your experiences and work with you to overcome difficulties.

Research focus

Castro, A, Kelly, J and Singh, M (2010) Resilience Strategies for New Teachers in High-Needs Areas. *Teaching and Teacher Education*, 26(3): 622–9.

Castro, Kelly and Singh interviewed 15 first-year teachers and analysed the strategies they reported using that seemed to make them more resilient. These included:

o   seeking help, sometimes from mentors allocated by their schools, but also from family and friends who were teachers, or other 'adopted' mentors;

o   problem-solving to resolve dilemmas or deal with classroom challenges, eg, through trial and error, consulting others, researching alternatives;

o   managing difficult relationships, including working with immediate colleagues or outside agencies (for example, working alongside those who were older or seemingly more experienced);

o   seeking rejuvenation and renewal, through maintaining interests outside school, making time to engage in the parts of the job they found most satisfying, and seeking out professional activities that they found fulfilling or stimulating.

Teacher voice

Dealing with the challenges of teaching

Natasha*:*   *If you're always teaching in the same year group you do have to do the same things so every term I try to plan a project that's new to me – that keeps me interested, inspired, and I can pass all that onto the children. If I'm doing something new, I'm more responsive to what the children are saying – I really listen. I am also prepared to admit that I don't know everything – including subject knowledge – and to ask advice from colleagues.*

Hilary*:*   *You need to be very efficient but also realistic about what you can do and make sure you do the most important things. You also need to work together with others, be prepared to compromise and be professional. This means being open and honest about what's happening in the workplace, treating everyone in a positive* and respectful way and not bringing in any personal issues. You need to have a positive attitude and go through the right channels if there are any problems. If there are things you have to do, and deadlines to meet you have to meet them, but if there's a problem you need to talk to your line manager.

Skander: I developed the ability to delegate to classroom assistants. I found it difficult to delegate to staff who were more experienced and considerably older than me. With time this got easier. I learned that I, as the class teacher, was liable and responsibility was with me. I had to reframe my thinking and accept that I had to delegate and lead. I also realised ideas can be recycled and that not everything has to be made from scratch. I have also learned to say no and realise that I can't do everything.

Kate: What I do is try and have at least one day off every weekend to focus on me and my family. For me, it's usually Saturday. Some people stay really late at school, but childcare means I am unable to do this, so I often bring my work home. The holidays are never my own. I'm either catching up on marking or planning for the next half-term. But the work I do during holiday time means that my classroom is prepared and organised and makes my working week much easier.

Mark: I learned to work on certain areas at a time and improve bit by bit. A lot of what you do as a teacher becomes automatic over time; you do very clever things that maybe you don't consciously realise. For example now I am very good at varying open and closed questions. It is however something I spent time working on during my first year of teaching. Now, I guess you could say I 'just do it'. Another area I can find tricky is using my teaching assistants effectively, not just as a 'run around'. I have good relationships with my teaching assistants. Part of this is maybe down to the fact I give them responsibilities and areas that they are in charge of in the classroom.

WHAT NEXT? FURTHER CAREER OPPORTUNITIES

If you become a teacher there are many opportunities for career development in the United Kingdom and abroad. You may decide to focus on developing your practice in the classroom, perhaps becoming an advanced skills teacher and/or studying for a Master's in Education. Or you may decide to pursue a career in school management, becoming a deputy head or head teacher. Alternatively you may opt for one of many teaching-related careers, such as:

○ providing specialist support to teachers and schools through advisory or consultancy work (eg, employed by a local authority education service or as an independent consultant);

○ gaining further postgraduate training for a specific profession, eg, as a speech and language therapist or educational psychologist;

○ working as an education officer for charities, arts or environmental organisations, heritage sites or nature reserves;

○ supporting the next generation of teachers by working in university- or school-based initial teacher preparation;

○ educational research at a university, most likely having completed a Doctorate in Education or Doctorate of Philosophy (PhD).

CONCLUSION

This chapter has provided you with an introduction to key aspects of the teacher's role and future career possibilities. It will also have helped you begin to consider some of the skills and qualities you will need to develop and highlighted a range of areas that you will want to investigate further. You should now be well placed to decide whether or not you are suited to a career in teaching.

 Progress checklist

○ Review the role of a teacher – is teaching for you?

○ Review your understanding of what 'being a professional' involves.

○ Talk to teachers about their experiences of teaching as a career.

○ Reflect on the qualities, attitudes and experiences you bring to teaching – focus particularly on team-working and resilience.

○ Consider the role you hope to have – in five years, ten years and more.

JARGON BUSTER

Academies: schools that have greater freedom over the curriculum and teachers' pay and conditions, term-times and the school day. They will have sponsors, which may include commercial organisations.

Advanced skills teachers: teachers who have some responsibility for supporting the development of other teachers and will gain a higher salary.

Faith schools: schools partially funded by religious organisations and partially by the government.

Free schools: schools funded by the government but free to develop their own curriculum and priorities.

Masters in Education: a postgraduate course provided by a university. This will typically involve supporting you in developing your teaching practice through research and enquiry.

Ofsted: the Office for Standards in Education; the body that carries out school inspections.

Teaching schools: schools that support the professional development of teachers across a group of schools known as a teaching school alliance.

 TAKING IT FURTHER

Arthur, J and Cremin, T (2014) *Learning to Teach in the Primary School*, 3rd edition. London: Routledge.

Provides guidance on a wide range of aspects of the teacher's role.

Eaude, T (2012) *How do Expert Primary Classteachers Really Work? A Critical Guide for Teachers, Headteachers and Teacher Educators.* Northwich: Critical Publishing.

Provides practical insights into how teachers can support effective learning.

Pay and conditions

www.education.gov.uk/schools/careers/payandpensions/
teacherspayandconditionsdocument

This website provides current guidance on pay and conditions for teachers.

Teaching unions

www.teachers.org.uk

www.nasuwt.org.uk

www.atl.org.uk

The teaching unions provide a range of guidance for teachers as well as information about the value of joining a union

---

REFERENCES

Bath, C (2009) *Learning to Belong: Young Children's Participation at School*. London: Routledge.

Day, C and Saunders, L (2006) What Being a Teacher (Really) Means. *Forum*, 48(3): 265–71.

Frost, N (2005) Professionalism, Partnership and Joined-Up Thinking: A Research Review of Front-Line Working with Children and Families. *Research in Practice*. Available at www.lx.iriss.org.uk/sites/default/files/resources/Professionalism_partnership%20 and%20joined%20up%20thinking.pdf.

Goepel, J (2012) Upholding Public Trust and Examination of Teacher Professionalism and the Use of Teachers' Standards in England. *Teacher Development*, 16(4): 489–505.

Hargreaves, A (1998) The Emotional Practice of Teaching. *Teaching and Teacher Education*, 14(8): 835–54.

Hobson, A, Giannakaki, M and Chambers, G (2009) Who Withdraws from Initial Teacher Preparation Programmes and Why? *Educational Research*. 51(3): 321–40.

Marsh, J (2003) One Way Traffic: Connections Between Literacy Practices at Home and in the Nursery. *British Educational Research Journal*, 29(3): 369–82.

Price, A, Mansfield, C and McConney, A (2012) Considering 'Teacher Resilience' from Critical Discourses and Labour Process Theory Perspectives. *British Journal of Sociology of Education*, 33(1): 81–95.

Tait, M (2008) Resilience as a Contributor to Novice Teacher Success, Commitment and Retention. *Teacher Education Quarterly*, Fall, 57–77.

3

Preparing to apply for a teacher preparation programme

David Owen

INTRODUCTION

This chapter provides practical guidance on making an application for an initial teacher preparation course. While recognising that recruitment requirements and procedures vary between routes and institutions, it outlines key elements of the applications process relating to:

○ routes into teaching;

○ gaining and learning from school experience;

○ writing a personal statement;

○ evidencing subject knowledge in English and mathematics;

○ preparation for, and taking, the Professional Skills tests;

○ resilience and professionalism;

○ the applications process itself;

○ individual and group interviews.

Scenario

PGCE interviews

Majid, Maureen and Mina sit in a teachers' centre waiting for the interview stage of their PGCE School Direct assessment to begin. It is ten days since they received their letters from the university/school partnership and they are anxiously reviewing their preparation up to this stage. It has been a long road. Each of them passed their English and mathematics skills tests – the prerequisite to obtaining an interview place. Majid was especially worried about his maths so he practised his mental mathematics using support from the National College for Teaching and Leadership (NCTL) at www.education.gov.uk/get-into-teaching

(further details at the end of this chapter). They're really pleased they got interviews and feel well prepared. The interview is led by a head teacher and university tutor. They begin their introduction, congratulating the group on getting this far in the assessment process. The interviewers explain the range of assessment tasks to follow. Majid and the others start the assessment... How did they get to this stage? Read on to find out.

WHAT ROUTES INTO TEACHING CAN YOU FOLLOW?

If you talk to a teacher who is about to retire, it is likely they qualified to teach in one of two ways. They will have probably completed a first degree such as English, then a one-year PGCE in primary education, or followed an undergraduate teacher education course for three or four years. However, the past 20 years have seen a wider range of options for entry into the profession. Many providers offer courses that are part-time, to attract applicants who are career changers or already working in schools. An increasing number of courses are based in schools, run by School Centred Initial Teaching Training providers (SCITTs) or via the School Direct programme. The 2011 White Paper *The Importance of Teaching* specified that, in England, schools should have an increasing role in teacher education. For example, you may now apply to a school or group of schools to train predominately in a workplace setting rather than at a university. Read on to help you decide which type of course may be for you.

Undergraduate teacher preparation courses

Many of the student teachers on undergraduate courses have dreamed of becoming teachers since they were very young. Approximately three-quarters of them progress to such courses straight from school or college. They value a full-time university experience and want to get a degree as well as learn to teach. The other quarter are mature students who did not go to university immediately after school and wish to gain a degree and train to be a teacher on a full-time course. Full-time degrees are completed in three or four years, with part-time undergraduate degrees lasting up to six years. These courses introduce you to both the subject knowledge and pedagogic content knowledge needed to be a primary teacher (see Chapters 5 and 6 for an explanation of the different types of subject knowledge). Many courses allow you to specialise in a particular area of the curriculum, for example mathematics, Special Educational Needs (SEN) or English, in preparation for a role as subject co-ordinator. If you have a passion for a particular subject, but don't want to teach in a secondary school, then such courses may be for you. Each year of the course will have placements in schools (between 120 and 160 days depending on the length of the course).

Postgraduate teacher education courses

As their name suggests, these courses are for students who have already graduated and hold a degree. Since 2006, a true PGCE course must include an element of Master's level (above first degree level) teaching and assessment, although there are still some professional graduate courses that lead to qualified teacher status without the Master's level credit. The former typically focus on developing pedagogic content knowledge and enquiry-based projects at Master's level. Increasingly, you can continue your Master's study with a university when you start your first teaching job. These courses are attractive to graduates, especially those who have school experience and have worked with individual or groups of children but want structured experience of teaching whole classes. They are designed for those who like to reflect on their learning, and improve their teaching through the use of enquiry and research. They are also appropriate if you have a passion for a particular subject and have decided on a teaching career after pursuing degree-level study.

School Direct

The teacher preparation routes discussed above are validated by universities working in partnership with schools. Teacher preparation routes offered by School Direct are different – the school is the lead partner in the training. You apply via the Universities and Colleges Admissions Service (UCAS). Places on School Direct routes are linked to employment in the school or group of schools offering the training places. School Direct works jointly with universities to provide aspects of the training programme, but government funding is not provided via higher education institutions. Such training places were first available in 2012. The Department for Education set a target of 5,000 primary and secondary entrants for 2012 and 9,000 for 2013. Actual take-up for primary places was approximately 80 per cent of the total in June 2013, and at time of writing was forecast to increase for 2014 entry, with schools bidding for more School Direct places than the Department for Education were making available. These places are attractive to those who know which area or group of schools they wish to work in. Salaried School Direct participants are paid as unqualified teachers. Unsalaried School Direct participants must pay for their course just like PGCE students and are similarly eligible for bursaries and tuition fee loans.

Overseas training programme

The overseas training programme (OTP) is a conversion course for teachers trained outside the European Economic Area. Teachers qualified in Australia, Canada, New Zealand and the USA are now recognised as qualified teachers in England, but teachers from other countries need to work in school and be assessed against the Qualified Teacher Status (QTS) Standards before being awarded this status.

The assessment-only route to QTS

The assessment-only route was introduced in 2011 for very experienced graduate teachers who have taught in more than one school and have taught across the primary age range. This pathway does not involve any training, preparation or educational activities in school or at a university. The completion of the application form and its assessment by a higher education institution is the main requirement for experienced teachers. This route is not needed for graduates to work in free schools or academies.

Research focus

Review of national teacher education models – plans for the twenty-first century

Tryggvason, M-T (2009) Why is Finnish Teacher Education Successful? Some Goals Finnish Teacher Educators have for their Teaching. *European Journal of Teacher Education*, 32(4): 369–82.

In recent years, Finnish research-based teaching, according to international surveys, has led to excellent results. Previous research has demonstrated that teacher education has often had difficulties in incorporating theory into practice, and that the effects of teacher education on the prior beliefs and views on teaching and learning of student teachers have been weak. Tryggvason researched how the Finnish teacher education system deals with these problems by investigating the current goals Finnish teacher educators have for their own teaching in theoretical courses. A total of 18 teacher educators were interviewed in five focus groups about different teacher education programmes in Finland. The interview results showed that Finnish teacher educators transmit theoretical and pedagogical aspects by using them in their own teaching, which is research based. They also aim to educate reflective and enquiring teachers by using a variety of pedagogical techniques in their own teaching. The role the Finnish teacher educators are said to play can be helpful in influencing prospective teachers' behaviour and thinking.

Reflective task

○   What do you want to gain from the university-based part of your preparation?

○   How might using and doing research enhance your development as a teacher?

○   How would you want to be assessed by school staff and university staff during your preparation programme?

Finding out more about primary teaching: which route is right for you?

There are many different ways into teaching and many variations within each route. If you haven't already, you need to do some research! The following are some good places to start.

1.   The Teaching Agency website: www.education.gov.uk/get-into-teaching. This site gives a full overview of all the current funding and application guidance. You can use it to access the UCAS teacher training application portal.

2. *The Good Teacher Training Guide*: www.buckingham.ac.uk/research/ceer/ publications. This annual publication reviews all providers of teacher preparation programmes and gives details of 'league table' positions, employability rates and other data that may be useful to help you choose a programme.

3. Social media networks, eg, *The Times Education Supplement* (TES) fora. The TES provide an online networking service through which potential and existing applicants to teacher preparation courses can discuss their experiences and progress through the admission systems.

4. Talking with existing primary teachers about their experiences. As part of pre-application school experience, ask the teachers you work with how they qualified, and their views on the merits of the different pathways into the profession.

5. Open Days. Universities have always run 'open days' to showcase their courses. Teacher preparation course open days will give you the opportunity to talk with existing student teachers, newly qualified teachers and their tutors. School Direct organisations (individual schools, Teaching School Alliances and Academic Chains) are now also running open days to recruit the applicants/future teachers they need.

GAINING SCHOOL EXPERIENCE

It is important to have pre-application school experience. You need to be volunteering or working in the kind of setting you wish to qualify in to gain the school experience required to get an interview for your course. Prior school experience is necessary for several reasons. Both you and the interviewing team need to be convinced that teaching is the right profession for you. Supporting individual children in a school setting, giving music lessons or sports coaching are different from being a class teacher responsible for teaching a wide range of subjects to children with a wide range of abilities. So work with individuals or small groups of children is useful but it will also be valuable to gain experience working with a whole class.

You may be able to gain such experience by contacting local schools, or by registering with the Department for Education School Experience Programme. You may be able to gain employment in a school in a support role, for example being a learning mentor or teaching assistant. Whatever your entry to school, make sure you get to work alongside class teachers and teachers who specialise in the areas you are interested in. Talk to the subject co-ordinators and to the SEN co-ordinator.

You need to see your school experience as part of the interview for your course. Familiarise yourself with current Teaching Standards (see Chapter 4), and be prepared to get an open reference (or testimonial) from the head teacher of the school. Admissions tutors will take these into account during the interview process. They will want to know that you are reliable, flexible, adaptable and professional. They will want to know that an experienced recruiter of teachers (such as a head teacher) thinks you have the potential to be a successful (or effective or good) teacher.

Head teacher voice

What I look for when interviewing for NQTs

As a head teacher the most important thing I am looking for in a newly qualified teacher (NQT) is confidence and a willingness to learn. No one expects the complete package but there is no getting away from the fact that from day one they will be taking responsibility for the learning and progress of a significant number of children in my school. It is perhaps an uncomfortable truth that despite the support you give them, the allowances you make and the responsibilities they don't have, an NQT is expected to do the same basic job as a teacher who has been doing it for many years, ie, teaching effectively so that children make good progress. The best NQTs are those that understand this very quickly, identify their pupils' needs and take responsibility for addressing them.

I need somebody who has the confidence to hit the ground running, to make mistakes and to learn from them quickly. I need individuals who can make an impact and whose individuality can quickly contribute to the bigger picture. When interviewing, and perhaps more importantly when shortlisting, I need to see something of the individual shine through. Too many applications are bland and uninteresting and consequently fall at the first hurdle. I want to appoint enthusiastic and vibrant teachers who can show that they can motivate and inspire. I expect to have to support them but I want to be reining them in rather than dragging them forward.

Peter Hooper, head teacher, Castle View Primary School, Matlock

Reflective task

o   What makes you an individual?

o   How will you stand out at interview?

o   What aspects of teaching are you really enthusiastic about?

o   Would your friends and family describe you as 'vibrant'? How could you communicate this aspect of your personality at interview?

o   Can you give examples of when your 'willingness to learn' has helped you develop as a learner or team member?

o   How would you explain what 'children's progress' is?

LEARNING FROM SCHOOL EXPERIENCE

Why are great teachers great? Can you remember an inspirational teacher who really helped you to move on in your learning? Many people can identify someone who is an 'expert' teacher, but expertise is often very hard to break down and explain (however, see Eaude (2012) for an excellent exploration of the expertise held by primary teachers). Teachers who are experts often find it very hard to explain exactly what they do and why they do it as their practice has become automatic and part of their everyday work. This is complicated by the fact that teachers do not work in isolation. Work is often planned as a team, or perhaps taught by a job share partnership, and supported by a range of teaching assistants. This makes observing what is happening very complex. And that's just the teaching! As Chapters 8 and 9 show, learning is complex too. So how can you make the best of pre-application school experience? It is important to:

○   be professional;

○   be confident;

○   shadow different roles;

○   focus on the children's learning;

○   talk to children about what and how they learn.

Primary school children not surprisingly have well-formed opinions about what it takes to be a teacher. Increasingly schools involve their pupils in the interview process for both student teacher and NQT interviews. NQTs have taught exemplar lessons to a group of pupils and may also have been interviewed by them. This practice has been extended to the interviews for initial teacher preparation programmes. School Direct providers organise interview activities where applicants are observed both asking children questions and being questioned by pupils. The interviewers' goal is to observe you working with pupils and also to gauge the pupils' reactions to you as a potential teacher. You are very unlikely to be asked to teach a lesson, although you do need to be prepared to take part in a practical activity, read with children or talk with a group of pupils. The box below summarises the views of a Year 6 pupil – they are very perceptive!

Pupil voice

What I like in a good teacher and class – my advice to student teachers

I like teachers who can control the class but treat us with respect. If the class is messing about no one can learn and everyone gets fed up. I don't like too much reading off the whiteboard – I want the lessons to be active. For example, use drama to re-enact history and use hands-on equipment to teach maths.

My advice to student teachers is:

- *get to know our names so you are more like the real teacher;*
- *be friendly but don't go over the top;*
- *always take your time to explain things simply;*
- *if someone doesn't understand, don't just repeat yourself, try and explain it in a different way;*
- *when you are marking work, give examples of how it can be improved;*
- *if you see successful work, always write an encouraging comment.*

Bethan Evans, age 11

Reflective task

- Who did you think was a good teacher when you were in primary school? Why?
- Why is it so important to learn the children's names?
- Why do you think children like feedback that helps them improve?

WRITING A PERSONAL STATEMENT

You need to stand out in any selection process. One way of doing this is to make sure your personal statement on your application form really shows your individuality. The National College for Teaching and Leadership (NCTL) set up an online tool to help create personal statements. While this is likely to create similar statements from different applicants, it is useful to review the questions they pose in order to create an effective statement.

1. Who or what has influenced your choice to apply to be a teacher?
2. Why do you think you will enjoy working with young people?
3. Why will you enjoy teaching your subject?
4. What did you learn about teaching through your experience in schools or other educational environments?
5. What can you offer apart from your own specialist subject?

(NCTL, 2012)

Question 1

This gives you the opportunity to introduce yourself and explain how you decided to become a teacher. You need to show your individual journey so far and demonstrate that you have a realistic and well-informed view of what it means to be a teacher. Strong answers to this question include reference to the different aspects of teaching: enabling learning, pupil support, child development and impact on the individual and society. Often a thoughtful review of experiences and people who have inspired you to teach will be effective – make sure that you review learning in a primary setting. Explaining that you were inspired only by your sixth form psychology tutor begs the question: why isn't this person applying for a post-16 teacher education course? Weak answers may include comments about 'just loving children' or 'I quite like the holidays'! Obviously these phrases are exaggerated and stereotypical, but they do represent comments that have appeared in individual personal statements.

Question 2

Here you have the opportunity to match your skills and qualities to the role of a primary teacher. You need to review what skills you have and how you used them when gaining pre-application school experience. Perhaps you have specific language, music or drama skills that you enjoyed using when working with primary children. Explain how you used those skills and why you enjoyed using them, as well as what you felt the children gained. Many applicants undersell themselves in terms of their personal qualities. If you have worked in another job prior to teaching, analyse how you contributed to the workplace. Did you use strong interpersonal skills, show empathy, demonstrate your self-discipline and organisation? If you did, give examples and show how you will enjoy using and developing these attributes in a teaching career. If you are applying from school or college, review your achievements to date and how you achieved them. Are you a creative or artistic person? Be sure to say how you will enjoy showing this side of your personality in school and how it will benefit the children.

Question 3

This needs some interpretation for a primary teacher preparation course. Are you applying for a generalist primary course that prepares you to teach across the curriculum? If this is the case, see primary education as a whole as your subject and explain why you will enjoy teaching the entire primary curriculum. Consider what the curriculum priorities for schools are at the time of applying. Do you need to explain how much you enjoy mathematics and teaching reading for example? Do your personal skills and qualities mean that you will really enjoy teaching the new primary science curriculum? Give examples and say how your journey up to this point suggests you will stand out. As introduced earlier in the chapter, many primary courses now have a specialism or specialist focus, for example the teaching of mathematics. You should review your enthusiasm and expertise in mathematics when applying for such programmes. Be careful to put your subject experience in a primary context – how did you work with primary children in developing their early mathematics skills, for example?

Question 4

This question may be answered throughout your personal statement as well as being a potential discrete section in your writing. The key word is 'learn'. This is very different from 'what did you do' when reflecting on your school experience. It is not enough to detail the number of days in school and describe what you did. Saying you 'listened to children read' or 'worked in an after-school sports club' is descriptive and needs to be followed up by an explanation of your insight into the teaching and learning processes involved in your interactions with children. For example, what did you learn from your focus on reading? How had the teacher organised this and why?

Question 5

This is about showing how much extra you have to offer to children and schools. You will have already explained why you have the potential to teach the primary curriculum and how you have the qualities necessary to work with primary children. However, many applicants will have this skill set. What makes you stand out as an individual? Examples might include the ability to speak another language, your experience of travel and how you might use this in your teaching, or the skills you have brought from a previous career. Talk to a friend or family member about this as many candidates take for granted the extra individual talents they possess. For example, holding down a part-time job dealing with the public in a shop can be seen as evidence of being resilient, reliable, able to deal with difficult people and an opportunity to hone interpersonal skills!

School and university admissions tutors read thousands of applications. A poorly thought-out personal statement can lead to rejection in such a competitive situation. The box below reviews, in a flippant way, some of the more extreme ways you can be rejected. General statements (numbers 1 and 2), reliance on teaching in the family (numbers 3 and 10), arrogance (numbers 4, 5 and 6), vagueness about prior experience (numbers 7 and 8), and a lack of commitment (number 9) can all result in your application ending up in the recycle tray!

Admissions tutor voice

Ten ways to be rejected because of your personal statement

1. I just love children.
2. I am passionate about learning.
3. My family are all teachers.
4. I will be a head teacher in five years' time.

5. The teachers in my school are rubbish. I will be much better than them.

6. I can teach now – I just need the badge.

7. I have spent some time in school gaining experience.

8. I am a regular baby-sitter and spent a few days in a primary school when I was in Year 9.

9. Teaching will fit around my other commitments.

10. My mother has already arranged my placements in her school.

EVIDENCING SUBJECT KNOWLEDGE IN ENGLISH AND MATHEMATICS

Evidencing your subject knowledge is increasingly important. Employers have commented on the need for primary teachers to have strong subject knowledge and reviews of the primary curriculum (Alexander, 2009) have commented on the perceived difficulty of being a subject specialist in all, or a range of, areas in the primary curriculum. Parents complain about the punctuation on wall displays during parents' evenings, and journalists bemoan the 'new' ways of learning mathematics encountered via their children's homework or parents' mathematics sessions. Demonstrating your knowledge of the primary mathematics and English curricula is therefore a good idea in your application and interview. As Chapters 5 and 6 explain, subject knowledge is not just about, for example, fractions and phonics. Pedagogy and inclusion are also important.

The following paragraphs explain how you can evidence your skills and experience in these areas.

Mathematics

Look for ways you can stress your personal skills and interest in maths in any way. If you have above the minimum qualification (Grade C at GCSE or equivalent), ensure you indicate this in your application and state how you might apply or develop your maths subject knowledge. Seek out opportunities during your pre-application school experience to observe and participate in maths teaching sessions. Reflect on the difference between the teaching methods used in your school experience and how you learned mathematics. You will need to be able to explain how teachers create age-appropriate learning activities to develop children's mathematical ability. Chapter 6 will support you in this process.

English

Your skills, expertise and enthusiasms in English and literacy need to shine through in any application. You need to be able to talk from experience about how children learn to read, and how parents, teachers and the children themselves have a role in early reading. Chapter 5 explains the background to early reading and phonics teaching – you may well be asked questions about this area at interview. Reflect on your expertise in English prior to your interview – if you have strengths or extra experience in English make sure you include this in your application. You will need to talk enthusiastically about how you read for pleasure and about your knowledge and enjoyment of children's literature. Questions such as 'What are you reading at the moment?' and 'What is your favourite children's book and why?' are worth preparing for, as teachers and tutors will only want to recruit applicants who can inspire children to develop and sustain a love of reading for pleasure.

PREPARING FOR AND TAKING THE PROFESSIONAL SKILLS TESTS

Student teachers have had to pass these skills tests before starting their course since October 2012. This changed the process of application and the preparation for teaching in a big way! The 'two strikes and you're out' policy of not allowing a resit for two years after failing a test twice certainly concentrated the minds of applicants, and a mini-industry of test preparation and coaching was born. The recent increase in the 'rigour' of the tests, implemented in September 2013, has also had an impact. So what is all the fuss about? You need to pass a literacy and a numeracy test designed to ascertain that you have the functional skills to work as a teaching professional – they do not test your knowledge of the primary curriculum. Indeed, early years, primary and secondary teachers all take the same tests. This section explains the format of the literacy and numeracy tests. Source: Department for Education guidance found at www.education. gov.uk/schools/careers/traininganddevelopment/professional.

The literacy skills test

The literacy test is a computer-based test divided into four sections: spelling, punctuation, grammar and comprehension. You have 45 minutes to take the test, unless special arrangements have been granted. The spelling test is taken through headphones.

Spelling

The spelling section is an audio test heard through headphones and must be answered first. This is the only part of the test that may not be revisited once you have left it.

The words tested are those that you could reasonably be expected to use in your professional role as a teacher; the words are not especially obscure or technical and are used frequently in professional writing.

You will not be penalised if you adopt American English usage when asked to spell a word which has an -ise or -ize suffix, otherwise you are required to use standard British English usage.

Punctuation

You are provided with a passage of writing. There are 15 instances of punctuation that need to be inserted. You are not required to remove or rewrite any sections of the passage. The passage may contain instances where punctuation is acceptable although not essential; non-essential punctuation will not attract extra marks, nor will marks be deducted.

Grammar

This section tests the ability to identify text that does not conform to 'good grammatical practice'. You will be expected to distinguish between text that makes sense and clearly conveys its intended meaning and text that does not. You will not be tested on your knowledge of grammatical terms, but on your knowledge of how to use grammar appropriately.

The grammar section requires you to construct a short, continuous prose passage. At four or more points in the text you will be asked to select the most appropriate choice for insertion to complete the passage.

Comprehension

The comprehension section tests the ability to identify main points in a text, distinguish between facts and opinions, retrieve facts and key points, make inferences and deductions, and evaluate meaning and statistics. The tests use texts such as documents published by various local and national government bodies, schools and the educational press. Extracts from websites and national newspapers are also used.

The numeracy skills test

The numeracy skills test is a computerised test covering three areas: mental arithmetic, interpreting and using written data, and solving written arithmetic problems. The test must be completed within 48 minutes, unless special arrangements have been granted.

Audio (mental arithmetic)

The mental arithmetic section is an audio test heard through headphones and tests your ability to carry out mental calculations using time, fractions, percentages, measurements and conversions. Each question is individually timed and the use of a calculator is not permitted.

On-screen questions

This section is presented in a series of on-screen questions, for which you can use an on-screen calculator. You are tested on your ability to interpret and use written data to:

o identify trends correctly;

o make comparisons in order to draw conclusions;

o interpret information accurately.

You will also be tested on your ability to solve written arithmetic problems that are set in a variety of situations and will include:

- o time;
- o money;
- o proportion and ratio;
- o percentages, fractions and decimals;
- o measurements (eg, distance, area);
- o conversions (eg, from one currency to another, from fractions to decimals or percentages);
- o averages (including mean, median, mode and range where relevant);
- o using simple formulae.

Student voice

Passing the test

- o Do the practice tests online and identify your weak areas.
- o Buy the latest books as they include lots of exercises for you to practice, and explanations of terms and how to work the questions out. (Not compulsory but the books helped me a lot.)
- o Ask friends or relatives to help you practice (eg, by reading out mental arithmetic questions to practice your mental calculations and get quick at doing them).
- o Be confident and trust in yourself!

When I booked my numeracy test I only had eight days to practise. I did the practice tests (one a day) and referred to my textbook, which I found really helpful. I started from having four questions correct to getting 12 correct, and although that means failure, I could see progress, especially on the mental arithmetic. When the day arrived I had the feeling that I was going to fail and the purpose of doing the test was just to get the experience so next time I would know what to expect. In comparison with the practice tests, the 'real test' was much simpler and easier (eg, the wording is easy to understand). When they handed me the letter I was shocked, surprised and proud of myself as I passed first time.

Micaela Da Rocha Afonso, 2012

RESILIENCE AND PROFESSIONALISM – PSYCHOMETRIC TESTS

Many of your graduate colleagues will take psychometric tests as part of applying for a job. The use of such tests in education has been somewhat controversial, but was championed by 'positive psychologists' such as Martin Seligman in popular psychology texts (Seligman and Csikszentmihalyi, 2000). Teacher training providers now have the option to employ such tests in selection for their courses. Why is this? There has been concern (as discussed in Chapter 2) that dropout rates from teacher education courses were too high and that teachers needed specific attributes to remain in the profession. It is thought potential teachers who are resilient may be more likely to sustain a longer career. Check with the courses you are applying for to see if these tools are being used.

The Resilience Scales Questionnaire (RSQ) is an example of such a tool. It has been designed to assess how you react to difficult experiences. You answer questions about how you cope with pressure and difficulty in five areas.

1. **Self-esteem**: Attitude to and perception of self in terms of self-esteem, personal confidence and competence.

2. **Optimism**: Attitude to and perception of the world in terms of optimism, fairness and future prospects.

3. **Self-discipline**: How someone manages their behaviour in terms of determination, perseverance and reliability.

4. **Control**: How someone systematically manages the environment and their ability to adapt.

5. **Emotional non-defensiveness**: How someone feels in terms of openness, tension and tolerance.

The RSQ has been constructed so that it is resistant to 'faking' and contains a 'managing your image' scale. The five areas above are seen as important in becoming a professional in a complex and demanding work environment. Holding an exaggerated view of your own importance or feeling worthless, expecting the worst in situations and having little optimism in how you see the world, lacking self-discipline or being too demanding or rigid in your behaviour, and being emotionally intolerant and 'grudge holding' are all seen as unhelpful ways of being or interacting with others.

Reflective task

Review each resilience category below:

○   self-esteem;

○   optimism;

○   self-discipline;

○ your need to control a situation;

○ emotional defensiveness.

How would you describe yourself against each category? How do you think this description will impact on your ability to be a teacher?

THE APPLICATION PROCESS

Both undergraduate and postgraduate initial teacher preparation courses now use the UCAS website. You apply for undergraduate courses via the main undergraduate route. There is a separate process for postgraduate courses, which is explained at www.ucas.com/how-it-all-works/teacher-training. You have two opportunities to apply. These opportunities are known as *Apply 1* and *Apply 2*. In *Apply 1* you can apply for three different programmes. You can use this system from the November in the year before you intend to start. If you are accepted onto one of these then you have completed the process. If you decline all of your three offers or are rejected by them then you can move on to *Apply 2*. In *Apply 2* you apply for one course at a time until you get a place or are rejected.

You register, pay a fee, select your choices from the menu, then complete a form to show your educational qualifications. You need evidence of maths, English and science GCSEs at grade C or above (or equivalent). You also need to indicate whether you have passed the Professional Skills tests. These will need to be passed prior to you starting your course. You will then need to detail your current level of school experience, work experience and paid employment. After this you need to add your personal statement – this can be the same for all your applications. You must provide two referees and UCAS will contact them for references.

INDIVIDUAL AND GROUP INTERVIEWS

Check the format of your interviews. Most interviews will involve some individual activities and questions as well some group interaction. The individual activities are likely to include: subject knowledge audits further testing your knowledge of aspects of the core primary curriculum; an interview with an experienced teacher and a university admissions tutor; any psychometric tests as discussed above. Group activities may be included to assess your interpersonal skills and your ability to communicate or potential to teach. These may include: group discussions; presentations to the rest of the group; and/or discussions with school pupils if the interviews are in a school setting.

Presentations

If you are expected to do a presentation at interview, make sure that you are well prepared. Ensure you are clear about the format of the presentation, eg, are you expected to use resources, make it interactive, use a computer or interactive whiteboard, stand up/sit down, etc?

○   Practise in front of family/friends and ask for their comments. Did you make eye contact with everyone? Were they interested in what you had to say? Did you vary the pace and tone of your voice? Did you express yourself clearly? Did you move around too much or fiddle with your hair? Did you sound confident (even if you didn't feel it)?

○   Practise in particular any unfamiliar words/phrases that might make you stumble.

○   Keep to time – very important – and remember that nerves are likely to make you speed up. Aim to strike a balance between being very familiar with the content of your presentation but not appearing to have learned it off by heart; write a few notes on a postcard to keep you on track (it also gives you something firm to hold).

Make sure you focus on the topic/question you've been given; tell them what you're going to tell them (introduction), tell them (perhaps three key points) and then tell them what you've told them (conclusion); make sure you don't say anything you can't expand on – you may be asked follow-up questions.

Admissions tutor voice

You'll be nervous – we appreciate that, but you'll need to convince us that you're committed to a career in teaching and will be able to respond to the demands of the course. Have you done your homework – for example practised your presentation, revised any 'rusty' areas of maths, found out what's in the news regarding primary education? Can you talk with knowledge and enthusiasm about your proposed career and the course you're applying for? Can you make links between your current knowledge, skills and interests and what you might do in school? Can you show us that you've been able to learn from your experience in school? Can you expand on your answers, giving relevant examples? And remember that we will be observing you from the minute you arrive! Are you on time? Do you talk to other candidates? What kind of questions do you ask?

CONCLUSION

Preparing to apply to an initial teacher preparation programme can be daunting. Many people wish to be a primary teacher and the sense of competition can sometimes be intimidating. However, with the correct preparation it is possible to reach your goal. The range of routes into primary teaching has expanded and may well continue to expand as School Direct develops further. It is therefore important, as discussed in this chapter, to research all the possible routes in the region in which you wish to study.

The most important factor in successfully preparing to apply is gaining pre-application school experience. Such experience gives you the raw material to write your application and personal statement, as well as shine at the interview. The increasing focus on subject knowledge is also intimidating for some applicants and the skills tests are seen as a barrier to entering the profession. The following chapters in this book equip you in rising to the subject knowledge challenge as well as introduce you to the all-important teaching and learning strategies at the core of successful primary teaching.

 Progress checklist

Feeling overwhelmed? Not sure where to start? Work through the points below and progress towards your goal.

- ○ In which country do you intend to do your initial teacher preparation? (You need to make sure you are familiar with requirements in that country for teacher standards, curriculum, teaching applications and routes into teaching.)

- ○ Check your qualifications.

- ○ Gain pre-application school experience.

- ○ Get references to confirm your school experience.

- ○ Pass the Professional Skills tests (England only).

- ○ Research your options/courses.

- ○ Write a personal statement.

- ○ Recruit referees for your personal statement.

- ○ Complete the application form.

- ○ Submit via the appropriate channel using the UCAS website.

- ○ Prepare for the interview.

- ○ Complete the interview.

- ○ Gain feedback.

- ○ Successful? Work on your individual needs prior to starting the course.

- ○ Unsuccessful? Act on feedback. Apply again.

JARGON BUSTER

Early reading*:*   *the reading skills and teaching and learning approaches relevant to children aged 0–5.*

NCTL*:*   *National College of Teaching and Leadership.*

NQT*:*   *Newly qualified teacher.*

Positive psychology*:*   *a branch of psychology that focuses on how people can live more fulfilling and meaningful lives.*

Resilience*:*   *the ability to withstand difficult circumstances and recover from problematic events.*

UCAS*:*   *Universities and Colleges Admissions Service.*

 TAKING IT FURTHER

Team Focus (2010) Resilience Scales Questionnaire. Available at www.teamfocus.co.uk/user_files/file/Resilience%20Scales%20 Questionnaire%20(RSQ).pdf.

UCAS Teacher Training (2013). Available at www.ucas.com/how-it-all-works/ teacher-training.

REFERENCES

Alexander, R (ed) (2009) *Children, their World, their Education: Final Report and Recommendations of the Cambridge Review*. London: Routledge.

Eaude, T (2012) *How do Expert Primary Classteachers Really Work? A Guide for Teachers, Headteachers and Teacher Educators*. Northwich: Critical Publishing.

National College of Teaching and Learning (NCTL) (2012) *Teacher Training – Application Form Assistant*. Available at www.education.gov.uk/get-into-teaching/apply-for-teacher-training/application-form-assistant.aspx.

Seligman, MEP and Csikszentmihalyi, M (2000). Positive Psychology: An Introduction. *American Psychologist*, 55(1): 5–14.

4

Learning to be a teacher

David Owen

INTRODUCTION

This chapter explores the nature of teaching and what primary school teachers do. It introduces the national curriculum in England and gives brief details of the curriculum arrangements in Wales, Scotland and Northern Ireland. Teaching is a commonplace activity but can be difficult to explain, so the chapter reviews beliefs about teaching and how these beliefs influence types of teacher preparation programmes. All forms of training involve meeting the Teaching Standards (DfE, 2012) and these are reviewed alongside the roles of school-based mentors and host class teachers.

Scenario

Robyn's class

Robyn, a primary teacher of ten years' experience, seemed to have a sixth sense that allowed her to know what the children were going to do well before they did it. Her class beamed at her as she entered the room. A barely noticeable gesture had the children eagerly moving towards the front of the class to sit on the carpet. Robyn spoke softly and introduced the work for that morning. The whole class was completely engaged by what she said. The teaching assistants, Jenna and Simon, were clear about the next step and led their children into exciting activities.

How do you learn to be a teacher and become like Robyn? What is the secret to being a great teacher? To answer these questions, we need, as in all good stories, to start at the beginning. When we talk of teaching, what do we actually mean? Everyone has been taught something through formal schooling or informal social and family activity, for example how to tie shoelaces, hold a pen, thread a needle or greet someone in French or Spanish. However, the familiarity of teaching as an everyday practice actually obscures the nature of the activity. Teaching, like any purposeful activity, becomes an unconscious act.

WHAT IS TEACHING?

You can think about teaching in different ways. Some would see teaching as a *technical* activity. From this perspective, learning to teach involves acquiring knowledge and skills that can be applied in the classroom. Such skills might involve the ability to assess a piece of work, teach a specific aspect of mathematics, structure a warm-up in physical education (PE), or conduct a parent/teacher conference. Others would argue that there is more to teaching than this and see teaching more as a *craft* that is best learned by observing and working with teachers. For example, teachers often talk about the idea of developing 'teacher presence' or of 'being professional' (something explored further in Chapter 2 and below). These kinds of things are hard to break down into specific skills as they rely more on relationships with others and how you conduct yourself. A third way of seeing teaching is as a *moral* activity. From this perspective, you can see teaching in terms of values and beliefs and recognise that teachers are constantly making choices about what to do, for example what to teach, how to teach, which children to work with, which resources to use. These choices are underpinned by principles about what is important. For example, what kind of learning will a particular approach encourage? Will it help children to reproduce what we tell them to do, or to think for themselves in creative and critical ways? Does a certain approach or resource advantage particular groups of children? Teaching as a moral activity recognises that all the choices you make are underpinned by certain values and beliefs. Many teachers would feel that teaching has elements of all three of these dimensions. Thinking about teaching as *technical activity*, *moral* activity and as a *craft* (Smyth and Shacklock, 2002) can help you develop your own understanding of the range and scope of teaching.

Reflective task

o   How do your current views on teaching fit with the idea of teaching as *technical activity, moral activity* or *craft*?

o   Talk to teachers you know about how they see their role. See how far their perspectives coincide with your own.

What and who does a primary teacher teach?

As a primary teacher you will be working with children aged 5–11. In this book we look primarily at the expectations for teachers in England. However, it is useful to see these requirements in relation to those in other countries. Considering alternatives can help you reflect on why requirements in England may be as they are, and reflect on the different values, beliefs and priorities that have informed them. Table 4.1 sets out the terminology used in England, Wales, Scotland and Northern Ireland to refer to each year group.

The curriculum varies according to the educational policy in each country.

Table 4.1 Year groups

Age at beginning of year	England and Wales	Northern Ireland	Scotland
3	Foundation Stage (non-compulsory)	Foundation Stage (non-compulsory)	Foundation Stage (non-compulsory)
4	Foundation Stage (Reception)	Key Stage 1, Year 1	Nursery (non-compulsory)
5	Key Stage 1, Year 1	Key Stage 1, Year 2	Primary 1
6	Key Stage 1, Year 2	Key Stage 1, Year 3	Primary 2
7	Key Stage 2, Year 3	Key Stage 2, Year 4	Primary 3
8	Key Stage 2, Year 4	Key Stage 2, Year 5	Primary 4
9	Key Stage 2, Year 5	Key Stage 2, Year 6	Primary 5
10	Key Stage 2, Year 6	Key Stage 3, Year 7	Primary 6
11	Key Stage 3, Year 7 Secondary	Key Stage 3, Year 8 Secondary	Primary 7

Curriculum overview

Each country in the United Kingdom has a curriculum framework that outlines curriculum subjects, assessment arrangements and, to varying degrees, how these should be taught. At the time of writing they are as follows:

Curriculum for Excellence in Scotland

The curriculum in Scotland is non-statutory and aims to support a flexible curriculum built around experiences and outcomes linked to the following subjects: expressive arts, health and wellbeing, languages, mathematics, religious and moral education, sciences, social studies and technologies. Details of Curriculum for Excellence can be found at www.educationscotland.gov.uk/thecurriculum/index.asp.

The National Curriculum in England

In England, the national curriculum from 2014 will include the following subjects: English, mathematics, science, art and design, computing, design and technology, geography, history, languages, music and PE. The curriculum includes 'Programmes of Study', which set out what will be taught in each subject. Details can be found at www.education.gov.uk/schools/teachingandlearning/curriculum/primary.

Most primary schools in England must follow this curriculum although some – free schools and academies – can devise their own curricula.

National Curriculum for Northern Ireland

The curriculum for Northern Ireland identifies a series of areas of learning as well as skills and capabilities. Areas of learning include: language and literacy, mathematics and numeracy, personal development and mutual understanding, the arts, the world around us, PE and religious education. Skills and capabilities include: thinking skills and personal capabilities, and the cross-curricula skills of using mathematics, communication and using ICT. Details of the National Curriculum for Northern Ireland can be found at www.nicurriculum.org.uk.

The School Curriculum for Wales

The Welsh national curriculum includes the following subjects: Welsh, English, mathematics, science, music, modern foreign languages, information and communication technology, design technology, history, geography, art and design, and PE. Details of the School Curriculum for Wales can be found at wales.gov.uk/topics/educationandskills/schoolshome/curriculuminwales/arevisedcurriculumforwales/nationalcurriculum/?lang=en.

Reflective task

Visit the national curriculum websites for each of the four countries of the United Kingdom to gain the most up-to-date guidance on the curriculum in each country. Consider similarities and differences between:

o   the aims of each curriculum;

o   the range of subjects included;

o   the extent to which teaching and learning approaches are suggested or proscribed;

o   recommendations for how to best support learning across the curriculum;

o   the reasons given for structuring the curriculum in this way (eg, principles for the curriculum).

BELIEFS ABOUT TEACHING

You will gather ideas about being a teacher from various places. Sometimes these are based on recent observations of teachers at work or from your own experiences of teaching. Often, however, they come from our experiences as learners. We have all been to school and been taught by numerous teachers. This means we have spent many years in what Lortie (1975) called the *apprenticeship of observation*, watching teachers at work and drawing conclusions about what is involved in good teaching and being a good teacher. Our ideas may also be influenced by the experiences of family and friends, and supplemented by how teachers and teaching are presented in the media. All these will influence what people entering the teaching profession think is important in teaching and being a teacher.

Research focus

Levin, BB (2003) *Case Studies of Teacher Development: An In-depth Look at How Thinking About Pedagogy Develops Over Time*. Mahwah, NJ: Lawrence Erlbaum Associates.

Research studies have tracked teachers' lives and explored how they arrive at beliefs about teaching and how these beliefs relate to what they do in classrooms. Levin, for example, studied the lives of four teachers over 15 years. She notes how these teachers' beliefs and practices were influenced not just by their professional experiences as teachers but by:

o prior knowledge and personal beliefs;

o the specific contexts in which they teach and have taught;

o personal relationships in and out of school;

o other life circumstances, eg, experiences with own children or their health.

Given the significance of these influences, she saw three factors as particularly important in supporting teacher development: the importance of support systems; opportunities for ongoing teacher development; ability of individuals to reflect on their teaching.

Reflective task

Take time to reflect on what you currently feel is important about being a teacher and what being a teacher involves. Consider where these ideas come from. Now compare your beliefs (and the sources of those beliefs) with a friend. Discuss any similarities and differences.

REFLECTING ON TEACHING

As you review prospectuses and website information about courses of teacher prepara-tion, it is likely that you will see references to being a 'reflective teacher'. What is meant by this will vary. When you begin your teacher preparation programme, your tutors and mentors are likely to encourage you to *reflect* on your practice. This means thinking through what you did (or what you are doing) and reviewing the decisions and choices you made (or are making). So think about what actually happens in relation to what you intend to happen, eg, how effective was a particular activity in supporting children to learn something? Why was – or wasn't – it effective? Did children face difficulties because of things such as: working with others; accessing resources; understanding what was expected? You will also find it useful to think of other consequences of what you did. What kind of learning was expected? Did they learn other things in addition to what you had expected? Were there opportunities for children to see what their next steps in learning were? You will also want to try and understand more deeply what is happening in an episode of teaching: for example, why is a child not engaged with learn-ing in a particular subject?

Reflection has been seen as a key skill in learning as an adult. Among others, Jenny Moon (1999) has explored the concept of reflection in higher education learning. Her specific area of interest is in how reflection helps professional development through reflective tasks and activities that support learning. Often this learning is structured by creating a portfolio or collection of evidence to show how the learner has grown and developed. For professional courses, participants are asked to reflect against competencies or stand-ards that define competence and professionalism in that area of work. The reflective tasks throughout this book are examples of tasks that may be in a portfolio.

Reflection is a type of mental process that we apply to difficult, 'messy' or complicated situations – exactly like teaching. What we are trying to do when reflecting is make sense of what we know, understand and feel. We may take for granted the situation that we are reflecting on, or have made it routine, just as Robyn had done in her teaching in our earlier example. Moon (1999) identifies the following aspects of reflection and has high-lighted activities to help analyse complicated learning situations:

1. **Standing back from yourself**

   Try writing about what you do in the classroom in the third person after you have been interacting with the children or teaching staff. Reflect on what you said, how much you said and why you said it. Where did you sit and why? Which children did you interact with and why? Practising these skills of reflection will help you develop your understanding of how children learn and how you support them.

2. **Reflecting on the same subject from different viewpoints**

   Talk or write about teaching from the viewpoint of the children, their parents/carers, or teaching assistants. Spend some time talking with, and observing, the teaching assistants in the schools where you are able to volunteer. Try to see what they see when working with the children. Do they have the same goals as the teacher? What is their standpoint on learning and supporting the children?

3. **Reflecting on the same subject from the viewpoints of different disciplines**

   Reflect on teaching from the viewpoint of a teacher, psychologist, social worker, police officer. See if you can talk with another professional who works with children in schools. What are their motivations in working with children and supporting their wellbeing? What do they think are the most effective ways to gain children's trust and attention?

4. **Reflecting on your emotional reactions to events**

   How does being in the classroom make you feel? At what point(s) did your emotions change during observing, supporting or teaching? How does what is happening in your personal life influence how you feel in a learning environment?

5. **Collaborating with others to reflect**

   Share your thoughts and writing with others to see what is the same and what differs. This is a really powerful way to develop your personal reflections on teaching. Talk your thoughts through with friends and family, with the people you work alongside in school, and listen carefully to their reflections. This will deepen your understanding of different aspects of teaching.

MODELS OF INITIAL TEACHER PREPARATION

Chapter 3 introduced you to different routes into teaching. In this chapter we consider the kinds of support these different routes will provide so that you can make an informed decision about the kind of route that is most suited to you. Institutions have developed different approaches to preparing teachers. Preparation has been seen as an apprenticeship, or based on developing as a reflective practitioner or on the development of subject knowledge and use of research. Although there is strong guidance on teacher preparation being led by schools, you will still see a variation in the approach used by different institutions and organisations. The following accounts explain how different approaches to teacher preparation help their participants to learn to be teachers.

Teacher voice

Routes into teaching

School Direct QTS (qualified teacher status) programme – an apprenticeship approach

I chose a schools-based route that solely focused on meeting the Teachers' Standards. I didn't want any academic credit, a Master's degree or feel the need to write written assignments. My School Direct route led me to attend courses run by the secondary school who co-ordinated the primary school I worked in. I started the course and worked in the school as a teaching assistant. I didn't have to research much – the course was run in a CPD [continuing professional development] centre and I was given some booklets about behaviour management and lesson planning. I learned through watching my class teacher and talking with her. I did get to meet some of the other participants at CPD sessions and at review meetings at the end of term.

BA in primary education with QTS – a reflective practitioner approach

I studied a BA primary education route straight after leaving sixth form college. At the beginning of the course we were encouraged to reflect on our development as learners and explore the attitudes to school we had brought with us at the start of the course. I was encouraged to reflect on my experiences in school on placement both at the time and after the placement. The course was designed to help me reflect 'on the job' while on placement – through the use of written evaluations and debrief discussions with a mentor – and also reflect with other participants on our learning across a range of schools.

PGCE with QTS at Master's level – a research-based approach

I worked as a teaching assistant before doing a PGCE course. My degree was in sports science and I was keen to apply some of my expertise in teaching. I was introduced to research in my PGCE early on and focused on collecting data about children's learning in school. I researched how children could be supported in enhancing their classroom talk. I reviewed how I used questioning during my first placement to improve children's thinking in science. On my second placement I focused on issues to do with inclusion. I researched what changes I could make as a class teacher to the provision for children with dyslexia.

Routes into teaching are changing and will continue to evolve. Chapter 3 discusses this in more detail. All courses however must lead to QTS. This is defined by the content of eight Teachers' Standards (DfE, 2012) and a requirement to have high standards of personal and professional conduct (see Figure 4.1). The approach to evidencing these standards varies but generally involves reflective activity to complete:

○   a training plan (for apprenticeship-style preparation programmes);

○   a professional development portfolio (for reflective practitioner programmes);

○   the completion of academic coursework at Master's level (for research-based programmes);

○   or a combination of the above activities.

Figure 4.1 shows the relationship between learning in school, university and independent study, and personal reflection. The learning in school will be supported by a mentor who is an experienced teacher. Work at university will be supported by a tutor. Both will be able to guide your personal and professional reflection.

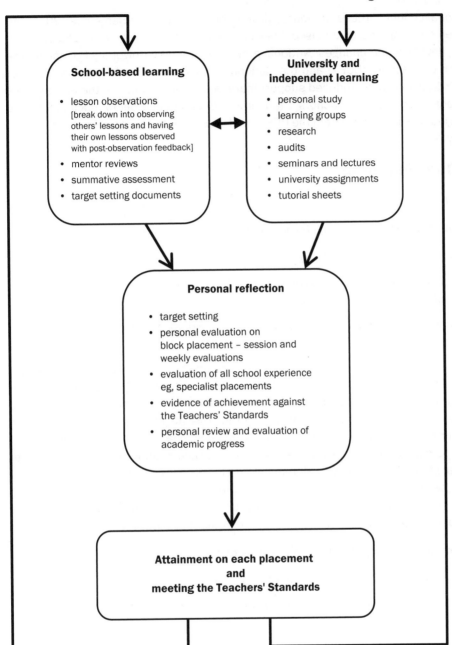

Figure 4.1 Cycle of progress towards QTS (SHU, 2012)

TEACHERS' STANDARDS

The Teachers' Standards are explained below. Each statement refers to an expectation of what a qualified teacher must do as part of their everyday work. The Standards are divided into two parts. The first section explains the demands of classroom teaching; the second attempts to define the behaviours and attitudes that are part of appropriate professional conduct. These Standards have been in place since September 2012 and have been questioned and criticised. They may develop and change as public policy on teaching develops and changes. National groups such as the University Council for the Education of Teachers (UCET) and the National Association for School Based Teacher Trainers (NASBTT) have produced support materials to make sense of these Standards for student teachers. The Teachers' Standards are reproduced below. Each is followed by brief guidance that draws from the UCET and NASBTT materials (see Higher Education Academy, 2012).

Part One: Teaching

A teacher must:

TS1 Set high expectations which inspire, motivate and challenge pupils

○   *establish a safe and stimulating environment for pupils, rooted in mutual respect*

○   *set goals that stretch and challenge pupils of all backgrounds, abilities and dispositions*

○   *demonstrate consistently the positive attitudes, values and behaviour which are expected of pupils.*

In the context of the primary classroom, this means creating an environment that is centred on learning. Whether it is in the classroom, or during learning experiences outside the classroom, after-school activities or any informal interaction with children, you need to set the highest expectations for your children. This might be shown by you talking about your own excitement in learning and overcoming challenges, or through the kind of work you expect the children who struggle in a particular subject to do. You need to develop a good relationship with all the children in your class and see them as individuals who can develop. Teaching is a really busy job and you are observed by others all the time – so you need to show that you respect colleagues, parents and other adults as well as respecting the children. It goes without saying that enthusiasm is crucial.

TS2 Promote good progress and outcomes by pupils

○   *be accountable for pupils' attainment, progress and outcomes*

○   *be aware of pupils' capabilities and their prior knowledge, and plan teaching to build on these*

○   *guide pupils to reflect on the progress they have made and their emerging needs*

○   *demonstrate knowledge and understanding of how pupils learn and how this impacts on teaching*

○   *encourage pupils to take a responsible and conscientious attitude to their own work and study.*

Teaching is all about progress. If you can help individuals and groups of children learn something new then you are doing your job. The skills to develop are working with your teacher/teaching colleagues to assess what the children can do at the start of a topic and then design a teaching programme to support their learning. This process needs to involve the children – so during your pre-application school experience you may see teachers asking children to assess what they know already. Teachers keep detailed ongoing records of children's achievement and development. Through your teacher preparation you will learn how to use these assessments to set the right type and level of task for the individuals in your class.

TS3 Demonstrate good subject and curriculum knowledge

○   *have a secure knowledge of relevant subject(s) and curriculum areas, foster & maintain pupils' interest in the subject, and address misunderstandings*

○   *demonstrate a critical understanding of developments in the subject and curriculum areas, and promote the value of scholarship*

○   *demonstrate an understanding of and take responsibility for promoting high standards of literacy, articulacy and the correct use of standard English, whatever the teacher's specialist subject*

○   *if teaching early reading, demonstrate a clear understanding of systematic synthetic phonics*

○   *if teaching early mathematics, demonstrate a clear understanding of appropriate teaching strategies.*

There used to be a saying that *primary teachers teach children, secondary teachers teach subjects.* This was never really true but the current standards certainly reinforce the importance of subject knowledge in primary education (see Chapters 5 and 6). As you develop as a student teacher, you will need to constantly develop your subject knowledge, eg, your knowledge about language and literature, and your curriculum knowledge, eg, your knowledge of how to assess children in PE or geography. This will enable you to pick out what you and the children will find interesting and exciting in all subjects and will also, with time, enable you to anticipate the common mistakes learners make when facing a new challenge in a particular subject area. This standard makes it clear that you need to be a lifelong learner in terms of your own subject knowledge. This may mean attending courses, becoming part of online professional networks via Twitter or other social media, and 'offline' networking with other primary teachers to share and develop innovative curricular developments. It also means you need to model excellent communication and mathematical skills in your professional life. This standard has specific guidance for primary teachers about subject knowledge in early reading and early mathematics:

In relation to early reading:

Primary student-teachers draw on their very strong understanding of synthetic systematic phonics and its role in teaching and assessing reading and writing to teach literacy very effectively across the age-phases they are training to teach.

In relation to early mathematics:

Primary student-teachers draw on their very strong knowledge and understanding of the principles and practices of teaching early mathematics to select and employ highly effective teaching strategies across the age-ranges they are training to teach.

Chapters 5 and 6 provide further guidance on the range and scope of subject knowledge you will need to develop in English and mathematics.

TS4 Plan and teach well-structured lessons

o   *impart knowledge and develop understanding through effective use of lesson time*

o   *promote a love of learning and children's intellectual curiosity*

o   *set homework and plan other out-of-class activities to consolidate and extend the knowledge and understanding pupils have acquired*

o   *reflect systematically on the effectiveness of lessons and approaches to teaching*

o   *contribute to the design and provision of an engaging curriculum within the relevant subject area(s).*

This standard focuses on the idea that learning can be broken down into separate 'chunks' and that the school day is separated into separate lessons. This is not always the case but the principle remains that teacher-directed activity will be present and that children-led activity will be planned. Over the course of your initial teacher preparation, you will gain the knowledge and experience to develop and create exciting lessons. Chapters 5–8 review some approaches to doing this.

It is worth talking with teachers and teaching assistants about homework. What is the policy in their school or their specific year group? Primary teachers and researchers are unsure about the effectiveness of homework in cementing and developing learning: in some primary schools homework is optional, in some it takes the form of online learning in English and mathematics and is specifically tailored to the needs of individual children.

Reflection is important here: how do you know if the lesson has been successful? You will learn to be systematic in being clear about the perceived impact of your teaching on children's progress, engagement and overall development. You may get the chance to influence what and how the children are learning. Do not underestimate what you can contribute from your personal and professional experience. Finally, investigate the extent to which planning for lessons happens in teams in the schools you visit.

TS5 Adapt teaching to respond to the strengths and needs of all pupils

o   *know when and how to differentiate appropriately, using approaches which enable pupils to be taught effectively*

o   *have a secure understanding of how a range of factors can inhibit pupils' ability to learn, and how best to overcome these*

o   *demonstrate an awareness of the physical, social and intellectual development of children, and know how to adapt teaching to support pupils' education at different stages of development*

o   *have a clear understanding of the needs of all pupils, including those with special educational needs; those of high ability; those with English as an additional language; those with disabilities; and be able to use and evaluate distinctive teaching approaches to engage and support them.*

Chapter 9 explains how teachers work to be inclusive in their provision for all children in their care. TS5 focuses on being inclusive and meeting the needs of all children. It builds on the earlier standards – once you know the children well you can start to adapt what you teach to their strengths and specific needs. Adapting your teaching is known as 'differentiation' – creating different work or levels of support for individuals or groups of children. You will learn that there is a wide range of social, emotional and physical barriers to achievement. For example, lack of confidence in spoken communication at the start of school can be a barrier to learning. Experienced teachers realise this and plan for a wide range of activities in a language-rich environment (see Chapter 5). This standard also recognises the importance of having a good knowledge of child development. This knowledge will support you in choosing age-appropriate ways of learning, for example knowing when to introduce more abstract concepts such as algebra in mathematics and when to focus on more concrete ideas. We live in a diverse society and it is a teacher's responsibility to meet the learning needs of all the children in the class. Chapter 9 explains inclusive approaches to teaching all children, with a specific focus on those whose first language is not English and those with Special Educational Needs.

TS6 Make accurate and productive use of assessment

○ *know and understand how to assess the relevant subject and curriculum areas, including statutory assessment requirements*

○ *make use of formative and summative assessment to secure pupils' progress*

○ *use relevant data to monitor progress, set targets and plan subsequent lessons*

○ *give pupils regular feedback, both orally and through accurate marking, and encourage pupils to respond to the feedback.*

Assessment is sometimes seen as the bane of teachers' lives; marking, report-writing and target-setting are time-consuming but necessary tasks. You will learn about the expected levels of attainment for each year group (although you will find wide variation within your class) and about compulsory tests and assessments. The key objective is to support children in progressing – widening and deepening their knowledge, understanding and skills. The most effective forms of assessment for this are formative. This means providing oral and written feedback as new learning is introduced. This also gives you the opportunity to adapt your own teaching and to evaluate your own success. Summative assessment happens at the end of a topic or series of lessons. You can use this to compare the attainment of children to others in the class, school or national attainment average, and summative attainment is used to report to parents. It is worth asking to see a school's assessment policy – this will help you understand how this standard is met in reality.

TS7 Manage behaviour effectively to ensure a good and safe learning environment

○ *have clear rules and routines for behaviour in classrooms, and take responsibility for promoting good and courteous behaviour both in classrooms and around the school, in accordance with the school's behaviour policy*

○ *have high expectations of behaviour, and establish a framework for discipline with a range of strategies, using praise, sanctions and rewards consistently and fairly* o   *manage classes effectively, using approaches which are appropriate to pupils' needs in order to involve and motivate them*

o   *maintain good relationships with pupils, exercise appropriate authority, and act decisively when necessary.*

Behaviour is a concern for all those who are preparing to become a teacher. Each school you work in will have a behaviour policy and you will be able to see the rules and routines that teachers develop from this. You will learn to apply the rules and routines fairly in order to support learning. The routines often focus on appropriate 'behaviour for learning' as explained in Chapter 8. It is worth discussing what interventions teachers may use. These range from a simple but effective 'look', to reminders of class rules, to more assertive challenges or final removal of a child from a particular situation. Classroom assistants and teachers will be able to explain the policies in detail using examples from their experience.

TS8 Fulfil wider professional responsibilities

o   *make a positive contribution to the wider life and ethos of the school*

o   *develop effective professional relationships with colleagues, knowing how and when to draw on advice and specialist support*

o   *deploy support staff effectively*

o   *take responsibility for improving teaching through appropriate professional development, responding to advice and feedback from colleagues*

o   *communicate effectively with parents with regard to pupils' achievements and well-being.*

As mentioned in Chapter 2, there is so much more to being a teacher than staying in the classroom or supervising children outdoors. You will become a professional who is part of a close-knit team. You need to build relationships with colleagues within your school. You will need leadership and management skills to get the best from support staff, and strong communication skills to work with the wide range of people in school. You need to continue your reflective practice outside the classroom and be prepared to attend courses, visit other schools and receive feedback from colleagues. You will learn to work closely with parents, for example at parents' evenings and one-to-one meetings. Chapter 2 provides further details on these wider professional roles.

Part Two: Personal and Professional Conduct

Teachers uphold public trust in the profession and maintain high standards of ethics and behaviour, within and outside school, by:

o   *treating pupils with dignity, building relationships rooted in mutual respect, and at all times observing proper boundaries appropriate to a teacher's professional position*

o   *having regard for the need to safeguard pupils' well-being, in accordance with statutory provisions* o   *showing tolerance of and respect for the rights of others*

o   *not undermining fundamental British values, including democracy, the rule of law, individual liberty and mutual respect, and tolerance of those with different faiths and beliefs*

o   *ensuring that personal beliefs are not expressed in ways which exploit pupils' vulnerability or might lead them to break the law.*

Teachers must have proper and professional regard for the ethos, policies and practices of the school in which they teach, and maintain high standards in their own attendance and punctuality.

Teachers must have an understanding of, and always act within, the statutory frameworks which set out their professional duties and responsibilities.

This section of the Standards focuses on personal and professional conduct and gives explicit guidance on what would appear to be 'common sense' values. The statement about British values, however, needs some unpicking as the focus is on respect for individuals and tolerance for the wide range of faiths and beliefs in communities across the country. An important aspect of this section of the Standards is the focus on safeguarding children. Whenever you are in school, you need be fully aware of the school's safeguarding policy. If a child discloses anything that causes you concern regarding safeguarding:

o   do not question the child or their parents;

o   do not promise confidentiality;

o   pass on any concerns to your host class teacher who will then inform the child protection liaison teacher;

o   avoid commenting but say that you will pass on the information to a senior colleague.

If you are accepted for a course of initial teacher preparation, it is likely you will be required to sign a document agreeing that you will be professional at all times. A sample agreement is provided below. As, you will see, the focus is on acting as a responsible and professional student teacher in a busy workplace – a potential change of role from being a school, college or university student in a flexible study environment.

Sample professionalism agreement

o   I understand that being given the opportunity to work in a partner school/college places professional responsibility on me to abide by the professional expectations of teaching staff in the schools/colleges where I am placed.

○   I will notify the school/college of any absence using usual school procedures. I understand that unauthorised absence may result in the termination of the placement. I also have the responsibility to ensure the partnership office is notified as early as possible on the first day of illness. I will repeat this process on my return to school and ensure I have appropriate certification for absence/doctor's note as appropriate.

○   I will seek permission (through my mentor) from the head teacher, should any time out from placement be required for a reason other than illness.

○   I will demonstrate my willingness and ability to listen to and act upon advice and feedback from mentors and host class teachers at all times during the placement.

○   I will strive to be a role model for children and demonstrate the highest professional standards through my values, conduct and work while in university and on placement.

○   I understand the need to develop effective and professional communication with children and colleagues on placement and in university.

COLLECTING EVIDENCE TO MEET THE STANDARDS

Responsibilities

If you apply for a teacher preparation course you will work closely with your mentors and/ or tutors and class teachers as you develop as a teacher. The following is an example from a university-based initial teacher preparation programme, which sets out responsibilities for all the key partners in this process. This gives you a useful idea of how you will need to act as a student teacher. You will gain a sense of how you need to act as a visitor, a team member and as a trainee teacher who is given progressively more responsibility. It details your responsibility (the participant), your class teacher's responsibility and finally your mentor's responsibility – the teacher who is assessing you. Review the following sections and notice how often you are asked to provide evidence of progress against aspects of the Teacher's Standards.

The participant's responsibility

Student teachers will use school experiences to develop their skills and identity as a teacher. While on placement in a school they should act as a temporary member of staff developing professional relationships with colleagues, pupils and parents. The student teacher's priority will be in providing high quality learning for the pupils in their host class although, as they gain experience, they should also engage in the wider life of the school, undertaking further responsibilities as appropriate and agreed with their mentor, eg, playground duties, professional development meetings, after school sports activities.

Student teachers will:

○ prepare, teach, assess and record pupils' progress under the guidance of their mentor and class teacher;

○ ensure that planning is made available to the class teacher in advance of the session being taught;

○ attend school during the hours reasonably expected of teachers; eg, 8am–5pm;

○ if ill, or unavoidably late, will inform the school as early as possible;

○ evaluate their progress against the Teachers' Standards on a regular basis and prepare for review points by compiling a profile that demonstrates that the student teacher is moving towards satisfying the Standards for QTS;

○ ensure their placement files are available for scrutiny in school;

○ act upon advice and feedback and be open to coaching and mentoring;

○ evaluate each session taught and complete a weekly evaluation reflecting on their learning and achievements over the week;

○ attend school meetings, if invited, as deemed appropriate by the mentor and class teacher, eg, weekly staff meetings.

The class teacher's responsibility

It is essential that the class teacher is familiar with the needs of the student teacher on the particular placement in order to support them and aid the mentoring process.

They should:

○ during placement preparation days, induct the student teacher into the life of the class, and arrange a mutually convenient time to discuss the placement programme and provide appropriate class information;

○ provide the medium-term plans for the class from the beginning of the school year;

○ give advice about the general areas of work/topics to be covered from medium-term plans before the placement begins;

○ ensure that the student teacher has the opportunity to teach across the whole curriculum, and agree appropriate weekly timetables for the student teacher;

○ give guidance about the student teacher's own medium-term plans before the placement begins;

○ give guidance on the student teacher's session plans the week prior to teaching if possible;

○ ensure that the student teacher has access to records and resources they need;

○ check the student teacher's session planning is appropriate before they teach;

○ be available close by or in the room during all sessions taught by the student teacher;

○ give the student teacher regular advice and encouragement;

o   give the student teacher regular oral and, if possible, informal written feedback about strengths and weaknesses in relation to professional attributes, subject knowledge, teaching skills, assessment and recording;

o   support the mentor in setting realistic, appropriate targets; provide evidence for the summative assessment; and attend reviews as appropriate.

The mentor's responsibility

The mentor takes an agreed responsibility for guiding and assessing one or more student teachers.

The mentor should:

o   on the student teacher's first visit to the school, meet with the student teacher to discuss expectations and the placement programme, and also provide appropriate school information;

o   set dates and times for the weekly review meetings during the placement;

o   use the student teacher profile, including targets from previous placements, as a basis for discussion of the student teacher's needs to agree appropriate actions for the start of the placement;

o   ensure that the student teacher has been briefed well in advance by the host teacher about the work they are expected to cover and given necessary planning information, and ensure that all aspects of the student teacher's preparation for the practice are sound;

o   ensure that the amount of classroom contact and the level of work required of the student teacher are appropriate to their levels of skill and experience;

o   liaise with the classroom teacher and encourage them to give regular encouragement, feedback and advice to the student teacher;

o   carry out observations during the block placement or arrange for observation by others (all student teachers should receive a formal written observation report approximately every five days during their block placements);

o   check that the student teacher evaluates all sessions taught with reference to Teachers' Standards, and completes pupils' records and detailed assessment as appropriate;

o   give the student teacher regular oral and written feedback about their strengths and weaknesses in relation to subject knowledge, teaching skills, assessment and recording, noting relevant Teachers' Standards;

o   facilitate, where possible, any subject-based training requirements of the student teacher;

o   hold weekly meetings with student teachers, reviewing progress and setting targets with reference to Teachers' Standards;

o   give the student teacher encouragement where possible, but also alert them promptly to any serious weaknesses;

○ complete a Cause for Concern and contact the university if the student teacher is in danger of not meeting the Teachers' Standards;

○ carry out the mid-placement review and ensure the appropriate reviews and grading sheets of the student teacher profile are completed;

○ complete an end of placement review in consultation with the university link tutor and agree next steps;

○ complete the Summative Report Form in consultation with the student teacher and university link tutor.

Being assessed against the Teachers' Standards

Each student teacher should have:

○ a weekly review meeting with their mentor, to include regular review of the student teacher's files;

○ mid-point and final assessment meetings, to include a review of the student teacher profile, which includes evidence of progress towards meeting the Teachers' Standards;

○ a formal observation approximately every five days throughout the duration of the placement. It is expected the mentor will carry out all but one of the observations.

CONCLUSION

Learning to be a teacher is complex and is not accomplished solely during your initial preparation. Meeting the Teachers' Standards is the start of the process but your development as a teacher will continue throughout your career. Reflecting on your learning and development will continue to be important at each stage. This chapter has provided an insight into the nature of reflection and into how initial teacher preparation programmes support a reflective approach to learning to be a teacher. The next chapters will expand on this approach, focusing on the development of specific aspects of the teacher's role, starting with the teaching of English and mathematics, them moving on to broader aspects of the curriculum and the importance of being an inclusive teacher.

 Progress checklist

○ Download the current national curriculum and familiarise yourself with what infant and junior children are required to learn.

○ Summarise how you learn best.

○ Start a reflective journal or diary, in which you record your reflections on your journey towards becoming a teacher.

○ Research the School Direct and university-based programmes in your area.

○ Download the current version of the Teachers' Standards and reflect on your strengths and areas for development in the context of each Standard.

○ Find out how the school(s) in which you carry out pre-application school experience support student teachers.

JARGON BUSTER

CPD: Continuing Professional Development.

Differentiation: the practice of providing different levels of work for learners of different abilities.

Formative assessment: an assessment of learning prior to the learner completing the final task. The feedback is designed to support the next steps in learning, leading to a higher level of success in the final task.

Lesson observation: the practice of observing student teachers and experienced teachers teaching a lesson. The observation is written up, often graded against Ofsted criteria, and discussed with the teacher after the event.

Medium-term plans: the planning document that shows the progression of learning in a series of lessons.

Mid-placement review: a meeting between a student teacher and their school-based tutor to review progress and set targets.

PGCE: Postgraduate Certificate in Education

Profile, portfolio: a collection of evidence in a file which can be used to review progress against professional competencies such as the Teachers' Standards.

QTS: Qualified Teacher Status.

School Direct: school-led teacher education introduced in England in 2012.

Session plans: the planning document that explains how an individual lesson will be taught, learnt and assessed.

Summative assessment:	a record of how well a learner has performed at the end of a task, for example gaining level 4b in a Key Stage 2 mathematics assessment.
Summative Report:	the report describing a student teacher's final assessment against the Teachers' Standards.
University link tutor:	a link between a university involved in initial teacher preparation and the school-based tutor.

 TAKING IT FURTHER

Eaude, T (2012) *How do Expert Primary Classteachers Really Work? A Critical Guide for Teachers, Headteachers and Teacher Educators*. Northwich: Critical Publishing.

Department for Education (DfE) (2012) *Teachers' Standards*. London: Crown Publications. Available at www.gov.uk/government/publications/teachers-standards.

Higher Education Academy (2012) Final Version of the UCET, NASBTT, HEA Guidance on the New Standards for QTS. Available at www.ucet.ac.uk/4647.

REFERENCES

Department for Education (DfE) (2012) *Teachers' Standards*. London: Crown Publications. Available at www.gov.uk/government/publications/teachers-standards.

Higher Education Academy (2012) Final Version of the UCET, NASBTT, HEA Guidance on the New Standards for QTS. Available at www.ucet.ac.uk/4647.

Lortie, D (1975) *Schoolteacher: A Sociological Study*. London: University of Chicago Press.

Moon, J (1999) *Reflection in Learning and Professional Development: Theory and Practice*. London: RoutledgeFalmer.

Sheffield Hallam University (SHU) (2012) Sheffield Hallam University Student Teacher Profile. Unpublished document.

Smyth, J and Shacklock, G (2002) *Re-Making Teaching Ideology, Policy and Practice*. London: Taylor & Francis.

5 Developing subject knowledge in English

Karen Daniels and Julia Myers

INTRODUCTION

If you decide to become a primary teacher, an important part of your role will involve teaching English. English is a broad and varied subject that provides the focus for developing skills in speaking, listening, reading and writing. These skills not only provide access to learning across the school curriculum, but are also essential to independence, confidence and success in the wider world. In schools, much English teaching takes place in 'literacy lessons'. The term 'literacy' tends to be applied to skills in reading and writing whereas 'English' also includes children's understanding and enjoyment of literature, their engagement with multimedia and imaginary worlds, and their ability to develop as enthusiastic, confident and critical users of spoken and written language.

This chapter will provide an introduction to the primary English curriculum and what you will need to know in order to plan, teach and assess this subject effectively. It will begin by considering the key role of communication skills in daily adult life, before looking at the knowledge, understanding and skills in language that children bring to the classroom and use in their lives beyond school. Examples will then be provided of approaches to teaching speaking and listening, reading and writing. The final section suggests how you can begin to build upon your existing knowledge about language and classroom practice in preparation for your application for initial teacher preparation.

LANGUAGE AND LITERACY IN DAILY LIFE

Reflective task

Consider the last 24 hours and make a list of times you have used language to communicate through speech or writing.

- What do you notice about *how* you used language in different situations and how this language varied?

- Consider your use of screen-based texts (eg, websites, text messages, social networking sites, online games, etc.) as well as paper-based texts (eg, books, brochures and letters).

- Consider the differences and similarities in how you used these different texts and how they were organised and presented.

The use of language and literacy is embedded in daily life. For most of us, every day involves many interactions with a range of people. We chat with friends, send texts, catch up on news, make phone calls. In all these activities, we choose the type of language we use depending on the context. Although we are generally informal with friends and family, at times we use language in more formal ways, for example, during interviews and presentations or when we write reports, essays or applications. The language we find in the texts we read also varies in levels of formality, from the dense, formal style of an academic text to the eye-catching slogan on an advert or the concise instructions of a recipe.

Language therefore varies considerably according to the context in which it is used; we choose the language that we feel is best suited to the situation. Depending on where you were born and your experiences since, you may move between different languages or dialects, for example, choosing standard English for more formal situations but at other times relying on your home language or dialect. In deciding which language or particular words and phrases are appropriate to each situation, you draw on experience and knowledge about language developed throughout your life.

The use of literacy also varies across different contexts. We sometimes write with great care to be clear, precise and ensure high standards of accuracy and presentation. At other times we pay little concern to such details. When we read we may read in depth, taking time to reread, or glance at a text fleetingly or scan for a specific piece of information. Generally the different ways in which we read and write depend upon the nature of the text and our purpose for reading or writing. Again, we make choices according to our situation and needs.

Nowadays, for many people, texts are most frequently read and produced on a screen. The impact of digital technology has been to expand traditional notions of texts and literacy. Texts are no longer confined to paper and print but incorporate sound and image and movement, enabling instant connections beyond the page and across the world. Skills in reading are expanded to encompass the ability to navigate web pages, scroll, follow links and make sense of different forms of media. When writing we may use editing tools, incorporate sound and image, achieve a professional appearance in presentation and communicate instantly with the wider world. In contrast with its traditional focus on language to convey meaning, writing in many contexts is a process of design and media production.

Language has also changed to accommodate developments in technology, for example terms such as 'laptop', 'mouse' and 'gigabyte' have been introduced along with verbs referring to related actions such as 'surf', 'crash', 'tweet', 'retweet'. Words traditionally used as adjectives are now sometimes used as verbs, eg, 'to indirect' or 'to favourite'. These examples relate to relatively recent developments but reflect the way in which language constantly adapts and develops. Words and their use can change over time. Some words cease to be used and some change their meaning over time, hence the difficulties in understanding historical texts and the trends in use of slang, greetings and indications of approval (eg, 'cool' or 'awesome').

Acknowledging children's experiences of language and literacy

Children bring rich and varied language and literacy experiences to school. It is important for teachers to recognise and build upon these experiences in order to effectively support their literacy learning.

Research focus

Brice-Heath, S (1983) *Ways with Words: Language, Life and Work in Communities and Classrooms.* Cambridge: Cambridge University Press.

The anthropologist Shirley Brice-Heath studied the home language and literacy experiences of children from a range of communities. She noted how some children's experiences were very similar to those encountered at school while others' were different, and these children were consequently disadvantaged. Her work has been very influential in demonstrating that teachers need to be sensitive and supportive to the language experiences that children bring with them to school and find ways of acknowledging, valuing and building on these.

Marsh, J and Millard, E (2000) *Literacy and Popular Culture: Using Children's Culture in the Classroom.* London: Paul Chapman Publishing.

Jackie Marsh and Elaine Millard carried out a study into children's media consumption, investigating their use of television, film and popular music. They showed how teachers can provide opportunities for children to draw on these interests and experiences in the classroom to support language and literacy development.

Below you can see how one Key Stage 2 teacher, Ross Watson, has drawn on these principles, successfully building on his pupils' enthusiasm and impressive skills in gaming and digital technologies at home in order to develop their enthusiasm and passion for English in school.

Teacher voice

Drawing on and developing engagement with popular media

By utilising the inherent passions of pupils I try to design a text-rich curriculum where a community of empowered learning is fostered. Research into the interests of my students revealed that children were entering school with a wide range of digital liter-acy skills and practices. By allowing the children to lead learning, I decided to enable the children to create an interactive digital mystery game for other pupils in school to play. Actively engaged, children elected to work in groups for co-operative dis-cussion, writing and reflection. By breaking the mould of ability groups and allowing my class to operate within focused yet fluid ways, a culture of collaboration quickly emerged and children were able to construct a plausible, functioning yet vivid virtual world. Multimodal texts became woven into a larger narrative; play-scripts supported film clips, love letters linked characters to mysterious goings-on.

Engagement was not the only outcome for my class. Learners developed not only their ICT [information and communications technology] knowledge and skills through filming, podcasting and presentation but also their reading, writ-ing, speaking and listening skills. Subsequent topics saw children more indepen-dently creating personalised learning journeys via the creative use of research tools and innovative forms of presentation. Together, we had opened a door into new ways of learning and teaching.

Ross Watson

THE CURRICULUM FOR ENGLISH

The English curriculum presents speaking and listening, reading and writing as dis-tinct but connected areas. Each of these is considered below. In September 2013, the Department for Education released details of the new national curriculum for English, which includes the Programmes of Study and Attainment Targets that are to become statutory from September 2014. The national curriculum for English reflects the import-ance of spoken language in pupils' development across the whole curriculum. The docu-ment states that spoken language underpins the development or reading and writing and that teachers should ensure continual development of pupils' confidence and com-petence in spoken language.

You can find further information about the national curriculum for English by visiting www.gov.uk/government/publications/national-curriculum-in-england-english-programmes-of-study.

Speaking and listening

All children will bring a unique experience of language with them to school and as a teacher you will need to plan opportunities to enable children to build upon, develop and refine their speaking and listening capabilities. You will need to ensure that children learn to speak fluently and confidently, are able to listen carefully to others, and can use speaking and listening to work collaboratively. You will also need to recognise that chil-dren come to school with a range of prior experiences of language use, and it is import-ant that each child's home language experience is valued. Language variety may mean that you teach children with different home languages to your own. In many schools, children speak a variety of languages (Chapter 9 focuses more closely on the teaching of children with English as an additional language). Within any one language there are different dialects. These will stem from the language that children use in their particular communities and families. Language variety can be a stimulating and interesting area to explore with children, and can also equip them with essential knowledge about how language works.

The National Curriculum requires that teachers teach children to use standard English. Standard English is itself a dialect that differs from other forms in some of its vocabulary and grammar. To help understand how you can value the language pupils bring to school with them, and also support them in their mastery of standard English, the notion of 'appropriate' language use is useful. Standard English is required in more formal situations, so children need to learn when and how to use it in both its written and spoken form. This means that if you become a teacher, you will need to be able to use standard English. This may be assessed as part of the selection process when you are interviewed as a potential student teacher.

Teachers plan opportunities for children to use speaking and listening alongside reading and writing. You can see this in the following example. In Ben Tinsley's classroom, the children are engaged in learning that is very rich in talk. Ben plans experiences that provide the class with different purposes to talk, for example, in pairs and to the whole group, as well as taking on roles and using different types of language.

Teacher voice

A Year 1 classroom (children aged 5/6)

My Year 1 class have been learning all about pets. They brought in pictures of their own pets to share with the rest of the class. This was a topic that interested them and they talked about their pets in pairs, to build up their confidence before talking to the class. It was important that this was a subject that interested them and I had also worked with the children to set up a 'pet shop' role play area. This contained a number of toy animals and other shop equipment, such as signs, notices and other print materials you might find in a pet shop. The children enjoyed taking on roles in the role play area, speaking in role as customers and shop assistants and using associated language. This gave the children the opportunity to try out different 'voices' and speak to different audiences, trying out a range of vocabulary and conventions that we use in varying social contexts. I had been reading the children stories about Kipper (the dog). Their favourite is Kipper's Toybox *(Inkpen, 1992) and the class often ask me to read it to them, but rereading well-loved stories is so valuable to them! I set up a reading area that contained soft dog toys and a selection of Kipper story books. The children loved to spend time there reading the books to the toy dogs and to each other! So that the children had plenty of purposeful opportunities to develop their emerging writing skills, I planned for them to make texts for the role play area, such as posters that advertise the pets for sale and a non-fiction booklet called 'How to look after your pet'. These were for sale in the pet shop so that a 'real' audience could read them and know how to look after their pets.*

Ben Tinsley

Reflective task

When you are in school, listen to children talking in different contexts, within the classroom and on the playground.

o   Notice how the children's use of language changes in different contexts.

o   Notice when and how children use home languages and dialect and how and when they are encouraged to develop the use of standard English.

o   In the classroom look at the different contexts and activities provided by teachers to encourage children to use different types of talk and for different purposes.

The teaching of reading

The very fact that you have chosen to read this book, that you are holding it and have opened it with interest, says much about you as a reader. You expect to gain something, such as new insight or information. You are interested in the content of the book as it supports your aims and goals. You have certain expectations about what it will contain, how it will be organised and the nature of the information that it will provide. This may be because you are a 'reader' who uses texts around you as part of your everyday experience in order to gain information, and at other times, perhaps, purely to be entertained.

Learning to read is a challenging experience for most children. In the national curriculum, reading is defined by two equally important but distinct dimensions: word reading and comprehension. Word reading involves the recognition or accurate decoding of words on the page. Reading comprehension requires us to process the words on the page or screen in order to comprehend, or create meaning. Comprehension is a complex process. In order to support children's comprehension, teachers need to provide children with opportunities to explore, discuss and share meanings. Teachers need to ensure that children are provided with opportunities to hear and read exciting and engaging texts, both digital and book based.

In the example below, note how Saira Sajid uses drama and film to help her pupils explore characters, events and themes from a children's novel.

Teacher voice

A Year 6 classroom (children aged 10/11)

I am currently reading my class the book Holes *by Louis Sachar (1998). I have chosen this text as it is a very powerful story that can generate class discussion around such themes as friendship, injustice and authority. This story is very good for creating purposeful contexts for writing in different genres. I also know that my class are familiar with the film version of the story and so I plan to use this experience to support children's understanding of the ways in which written texts and films create meaning. I have a number of traveller children in my class, who can at times struggle with spoken and written English. I have found that by using film, with moving images, and drama, they can really begin to show what they know and understand and find ways to communicate which then supports their writing.*

First, I carefully chose the scene from the story where the main character, Stanley, arrives at Camp Green Lake. As readers we know Stanley must have done something wrong but we aren't sure what this is. I read this section of the book to the children and asked them to dramatise this scene in small groups. I used a popular drama strategy called 'freeze framing'. This allows children to explore one moment in the story. The children used gesture, body position and facial expression to communicate complex ideas from the text. This really supports children's understanding of the text and its powerful themes.

The children then developed this freeze frame into a short sequence of events. One child in each group used the film function on an iPad to film the sequence. The children watched their own film clips and then we watched the same part of the story from the film version. The children enjoyed making comparisons between their dramatised scene and the one in the film. The children then discussed how the features of the film, such as camera angle, setting, sound effects and costume, created meaning in the film version. They compared this with the gesture, voice and body position in their dramatised scenes.

This book also provides opportunities for writing in role. I shared a newspaper report of a recent event in the news with the children. The children looked at features of this text and then, in the role of journalists, produced their own newspaper report on Stanley's 'crime'. In order to do this well, my class explored the report's use of the active and passive voice and how this can be used to influence the reader's opinion in headlines. They then applied this in their own headline writing.

Saira Sajid

The use of children's literature

As adults, we can often recall favourite books and stories, but very rarely remember how we became a reader. The children in Ben's class earlier will probably remember the Kipper stories for many years to come! Saira's class will vividly recall the experience of Stanley at Camp Green Lake as the character's experiences were brought to life for them through experiences with print, drama and film. Teachers must seek to provide children with reading material that they will enjoy, broadening the kinds of texts they read while also recognising and building on personal interests.

Reflective task

○   Recall a story from your childhood that you loved. What was the story? Did you read it yourself or was someone reading to you? Can you remember why you enjoyed it so much?

○   What did you like about your story? How do you think that experience impacted on you as a reader?

The use of children's literature is central to any English teaching programme. Experiencing a rich variety of engaging texts not only provides children with a model of language, but shows them how reading can be a rewarding and enjoyable activity. As you prepare to apply for a teacher preparation programme, build up a store of knowledge of books by popular children's authors. This is not only fun but will support you in being well prepared to plan engaging and motivating language and literacy experiences. Teachers who read themselves and have an extensive knowledge of children's literature can more effectively support their pupils' reading (Cremin et al, 2009). You can get to know children's authors by browsing children's sections of book shops and libraries and looking out for shortlists for children's book prizes, such as the CILIP Carnegie and Kate Greenaway Medals or the *Guardian* children's book award. Useful children's literature websites are listed at the end of this chapter.

Reflective task

Find a book that you like and practise reading it aloud as a teacher would. If you have the opportunity, read it aloud to a small group of children – these could be family or friends.

- o Think about ways you can involve children and encourage them to listen or participate.
- o Afterwards, review how the children responded. Consider what was effective and any ways in which you could have improved your reading.

The teaching of early reading and phonics

Teaching children to read is a very complex process that has been explored and debated for many years. Some have advocated teaching children to read using whole books, while others have argued that we need to teach children very specific skills that they can then use to read texts. In practice, a combination of strategies is used to support children's reading and it is generally understood that different children learn to read in different ways. Teachers plan a range of activities to support children's understanding of and response to texts, while also teaching them the specific reading skills and knowledge they will need, such as skimming to read non-fiction texts, using glossaries and 'word attack' skills (strategies to read individual words).

In 2006, Jim Rose presented an *Independent Review of the Teaching of Early Reading* (Rose, 2006). This review led to recent changes in policy in the teaching of early reading in England. Rose highlighted the role of speaking and listening. As explored above, speaking and listening are prime communication skills, hugely important in their own right and central to children's intellectual, social and emotional development. (You can read more about the role of talk in supporting learning across the curriculum in Chapter 7.) Rose, however, highlighted the importance of children acquiring a good stock of vocabulary, learning to listen attentively, and speak clearly and confidently, arguing that these skills are the foundations of phonic work, for example, in building phonemic awareness.

Rose proposed that systematic synthetic phonics should be the prime approach to the teaching of early reading but that it should be set within a broad and rich language curriculum that develops speaking, listening, reading and writing. He also proposed that systematic phonic work should start by the age of five. There are different views on the best way to teach phonics (Dombey, 2010). However, since Rose's review in 2006, there has been a focus on systematic synthetic phonics, and primary teachers are expected to be confident and competent in supporting reading and spelling using phonics as the prime approach.

Reflective task

Review the following sources:

Dombey, H (2010) *Teaching Reading: What the Evidence Says*. Leicester: United Kingdom Literacy Association.

This booklet draws on research evidence to present a range of viewpoints on the teaching of reading.

Wyse, D, Jones, R, Bradford, H and Wolpert, M (2008) *Teaching English, Language and Literacy*, 2nd edition. London: Routledge.

This book includes chapters detailing a history of the teaching of reading, along with information on approaches to the teaching of early reading, including those reflected in current government policy.

www.michaelrosen.co.uk/index.html

On this website, the children's author Michael Rosen presents his viewpoints on the teaching of reading. There are links to a range of his poems (some performed by him), for use with children. Rosen invites children to submit their own poetry to the website and gives his views on the value of poetry for children.

o   What do different authors suggest are important in the teaching of reading?

o   Which approaches to teaching reading have you observed? Consider why teachers chose to use these approaches. Which aspects of reading were they trying to develop?

The role of phonics in the teaching of early reading

It is important to recognise that phonics is not a subject in its own right. Phonics is one of a repertoire of strategies that a child can use to decode (or work out) words on a page. Phonics is derived from the study of phonetics, or the speech sounds of languages. Teaching about phonics involves teaching about phonemes or speech sounds, and how these are represented in the writing system by the use of graphemes (letters or combinations of letters that represent sounds). There are approximately 44 phonemes in the English language (dependent on local accents). For example, the word 'ship' has three phonemes that relate to the three graphemes or symbols 'sh-i-p'. There are a number of commercially produced systematic synthetic phonics programmes. Most systematic synthetic phonics programmes, some of which you may meet when you visit schools, follow a very similar progression.

Reflective task

o   When you are in a school or talking to children, find out about the sorts of reading they like to do, at home and at school. Look at the range of texts they read in the classroom. Ask them about what motivates them to read and what they find challenging.

o   Consider the implications of what you find out for your future planning and teaching of reading.

o   In the classroom, look for the strategies that teachers use to develop: confidence and enthusiasm for reading; understanding of texts; reading strategies and phonic knowledge.

○ Collect examples of activities, strategies and texts that seem to be effective at different stages of the primary school.

The teaching of writing

Just as we often take for granted the ability to read, we may well have forgotten the challenges we faced in learning to write. Young children not only have to develop the physical control required to produce specific shapes or letters, but also the understanding that these letters represent sounds. Equally important, children need to acquire the ability to organise their thoughts in order to communicate meaning through the written word, presenting the content in a way that will make sense to their reader and be appropriate to their purpose for writing, for example as instructions, stories, persuasive texts or poetry. The teaching of writing is therefore concerned with developing children's ability to articulate and structure their ideas, their organisation of language (also known as grammar), punctuation, spelling and handwriting. In the national curriculum for English (2014), writing has the two dimensions of *transcription* and *composition*. Transcription includes skills such as spelling and handwriting, and composition involves the child's developing ability to articulate and structure their ideas in writing for specific audiences and purposes.

Providing purposeful and motivating contexts for writing

In teaching writing we aim to enable children to see themselves as writers. In order to do this we need to provide interesting and varied contexts in which children are motivated to write. Earlier Ben demonstrated how he achieved this through his design of the role play area as a pet shop, which was meaningful and interesting to the children, as well as being an appropriate context for the design of posters and instruction leaflets. In the account below, Chris Suffolk describes how she encourages her class to write by drawing on their experience of a visit to a castle and giving them a purpose for their writing.

Teacher voice

A Year 3 classroom (children aged 7/8)

I am currently teaching narrative writing to my Year 3 class and am using drama and speaking and listening to generate ideas for writing. The children have recently visited Warwick Castle and this has generated a series of lessons in which we have designed brochures for visitors to the castle. The visit has provided a suitable audience for the writing. When we returned from the visit we e-mailed electronic copies of the brochures to the castle so they could be displayed there for visitors. This gave the children an ideal opportunity to combine texts that were both factual and informative (providing useful information and history about the castle) and also use persuasive language to encourage visitors to the castle.

Following the visit, the class have become very interested in dragons and so I decided to use this as a stimulus to develop narrative writing. I printed off a number of images of dragons and we used these so that each child could devise their own dragon character. I read a story opening in which a dragon sleeps outside a castle, waiting for victims. The children were in role as the castle council, and held a debate about possible solutions to their problem. The council came up with different ideas, and settled on the decision to invite a nearby wizard to the castle to see if he could help. We used drama to explore the meeting with the wizard and his solutions to the dragon problem. The children then worked in groups to plan how the dragon problem was resolved. Their alternative endings were shared in a class book.

Chris Suffolk

Pupil voice

Why I like writing

I liked my dragon story because we could make our own dragon up. I like doing fairy tale stories too. I am most pleased with my fairy tale story because it was funny.

Brandon, age 7

I love making my own stories because you can make a creative one, and it makes people write more! I write my own stories at home. My favourite was my magic box poem and I am pleased with it because it took me a long time and I tried my hardest.

Carrie, age 10

Planning for the teaching of writing therefore involves finding ways to motivate children to write by providing engaging topics and meaningful and varied purposes for their writing. Purposes for writing need to be varied so that children gain experience of writing different types of texts. For example, if you look back at the teachers' accounts in this chapter you will see that children were involved in producing posters, instruction texts, brochures, fantasy stories, blogs and films. As well as writing on paper, they created digital texts. Using technology they were able to incorporate a range of images, achieve a professional standard of presentation and communicate with audiences beyond the classroom.

Reflective task

○   When you're in a school or talking to children find out about the sorts of writing they like to do, at home and at school. Look at the range of texts they create. Ask them about what motivates them to write and what they find challenging.

○   Consider the implications of what you find out for your future planning and teaching of writing.

Digital technology and its influence on ways of reading and writing

Given the widespread use of digital technology in the world beyond the classroom, many children have been using and producing screen-based texts from a very early age. In your classroom you may well find that your children are confident users of mobile phones, the internet, computer games and so on. The teaching of English provides an opportunity to draw upon such expertise and explore the opportunities provided by technology for engaging children in meaningful and exciting contexts for communication, for example, creating and using virtual worlds, planning and producing films and simulations, documentaries and games. Such contexts provide opportunities to reinforce key aspects of literacy that support the effective use of language across all texts. At the same time, experience of digital media cannot be taken for granted so it is essential to ensure that children who are less confident and experienced in the use of digital media are supported and encouraged to be critical in their response to texts. As we can see in Daniel's comments below, using digital technology is very much part of his everyday use of literacy. Notice how he lists reading and writing paper-based texts, such as writing a diary entry or reading a novel, alongside his use of digital texts.

Pupil voice

Daniel's literate life

I like to read on my Kindle and my iPad. I do lots of reading and writing on my Xbox360 and on the internet, like texting and e-mails. I have a pen pal and I write my diary too. I like Jacqueline Wilson books and Michael Morpurgo and I like to read things on the internet like the news.

Daniel, age 10

As a primary teacher, finding ways to inspire children to want to write is an important responsibility and a challenge, but support for their development as writers is also essential. Teachers use guidance, modelling, feedback, explicit instruction and discussion to help children develop understanding of how different types of texts are written and how to make their writing effective and accurate.

Progression in writing

In order to plan for children to develop as writers, you will need to plan for progression. This means recognising the skills and knowledge a child already has and planning to support them in what they need to know next. As a teacher, you will be responsible for developing the following aspects of writing, enabling children to understand the features of different types of texts:

o   organisation and structure of the texts;

o   vocabulary;

o   grammar and punctuation;

o   spelling;

o   handwriting.

You will equip them to adapt their use of language in order communicate effectively with different audiences. The following task is designed to illustrate the kind of knowledge you will need in order to do this.

Reflective task

Look at these four pieces of writing, written by the same child, Michael, between the ages of three and seven. Note how he has made progress in each of the following areas:

o   organisation and structure of the texts;

o   vocabulary;

o   grammar and punctuation;

o   spelling;

o   handwriting.

Sample 1: Train track

The text on the next page was produced by Michael (three-and-a-half years old) at home with his mother. He drew the train track, with wheels, and then added the letter shapes above. As he wrote he made train noises and commented, *Mum, look at them wheels!* Later, indicating the letter shapes he asked, *What does it say?*

Sample 1

Commentary

Michael's picture clearly shows the shape of a train track and the lines added around the outside seem to represent movement. The fact that he places his writing above the picture suggests that he recognises the role and position of a title. Michael's question to his mother shows that he understands that writing conveys meaning and is aware that he cannot access this independently. Michael has drawn the letters accurately although some are reversed. He may have intended to separate the letters into two groups (as there is a gap between the c and t) but his question suggests that he is probably not aware that groups of letters represent individual words.

At this early stage Michael successfully communicates his enthusiasm for trains and clearly understands that writing and pictures are used to convey meaning, although he is not yet aware of the use of letters to convey specific sounds.

Sample 2: Christmas tree

Commentary

Michael (age six) now successfully relates a short sequence of events providing an element of tension for the reader, by saving the cause of his excitement until the end of the

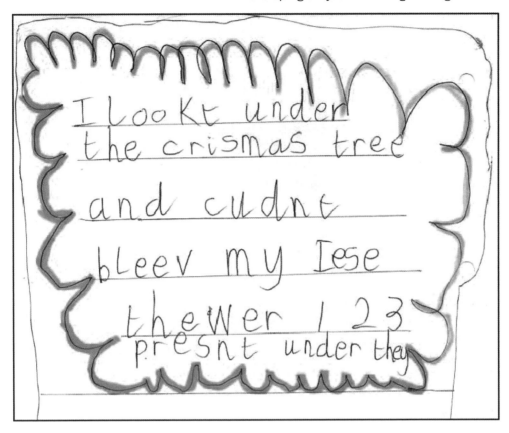

Sample 2 **Text:** (spelling corrected) *I looked under the Christmas tree and couldn't believe my eyes there were 1, 2, 3 presents under there.*

text. He conveys his feelings well to the reader, through his language (*couldn't believe my eyes*) and the individual counting of the presents.

Michael's text has cohesion, in other words it holds together well. He links ideas by using the connective 'and' to join two clauses. *I looked under the Christmas tree and couldn't believe my eyes.* Although not indicated by punctuation, this is a co-ordinated sentence, which is followed by a simple sentence (*There were 1, 2, 3 presents under there*). This contrasting short sentence adds emphasis to his surprise. Appropriately for a recount or narrative text, Michael's use of verbs (*looked, couldn't, were*) are consistently in the past tense.

Michael's formation of letters is accurate and he spells several words (*under, the, tree, and, my*) accurately. Other words are written phonetically; Michael represents the sounds he can hear in each word with sequences of letters, so that they can be understood by the reader.

Sample 3: Crocodile facts

A year later, Michael (age seven) produced this factsheet about crocodiles as a summary of his research findings from a school research project.

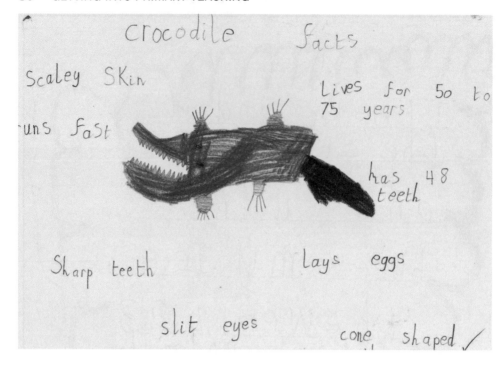

crocodile facts

Scaley Skin

Lives for 50 to 75 years

uns Fast

has 48 teeth

Sharp teeth

Lays eggs

slit eyes

cone shaped ✓

Sample 3

Commentary

Michael's literacy skills now enable him to gather his own information, process it and present it clearly, effectively and accurately. The text resembles a page from an information book or internet page in its concise and visual presentation of information. Michael has placed his drawing in the centre of the page, drawing attention to the topic, which is reinforced through his use of colour and a simple, direct title: *crocodile facts*. The positioning of short individual phrases around the picture suggest that all of these pieces of information are relevant and equally important.

Michael's use of noun phrases (*scaley* [sic] *skin*; *sharp teeth*; *slit eyes*; *cone shaped teeth*) and verb phrases (*runs fast*; *lays eggs*; *lives for 50 to 75 years*; *has 48 teeth*) rather than sentences shows that he recognises the value of presenting information in a concise and focused way. His choice of adjectives (*scaley, sharp, slit, cone shaped*) and adverb (*fast*) is precise and effective in focusing on relevant information. Michael's spelling is accurate and his letter formation is clear and consistent.

Sample 4: Homes text

Later in the year, Michael (age seven years and nine months) produced this information sheet about houses. This was related to a school topic but was researched and written at home.

Mexico:
Mexican houses are made from clay and mud. The clay and mud together makes strong bricks that makes the houses.

American Bungalow:
They have swimming pools in the gardens. They have tiles on the roves.

They are made from bricks and have sloped roves. They are really small houses and the bricks are kept together by cement. ↑
Bungalow:

Spain:
The walls are white because White reflects the sun to stop it getting hot in the house.

igloo:
Igloos are made from hard blocks of snow. The remaining holes are blocked up with loose snow. It's warm inside the igloos.

Tepee:
Tepees are a sort of tent. There made from bussbalo skin. The doors are circles.

Sample 4

Commentary

Michael has provided an informative overview of different kinds of homes and how they are made. He has presented the information clearly, dividing the page into sections to enable the reader to focus on each type of home. The sections are the same size, conveying that each type of home is equally significant. Each section contains a drawing to illustrate key features of each home and information presented in the style of a non-narrative report, as used in information texts (eg, BBC natural history website or in non-fiction books or encyclopaedias). Michael has shown his understanding of these features of this type of text, by writing in the present tense (eg, *are made from, reflects*) and using the passive voice (*are made, are blocked up*) to express information concisely, focusing the reader's attention on the features of the homes rather than the people who built them. He selects adjectives carefully to provide essential details (eg, *sloped, loose, remaining*). He also uses subordination to link clauses within a sentence in order to provide an explanation: *The walls are white because white reflects the sun to stop it getting to* [sic] *hot in the house.*

Michael's writing is generally accurate and punctuated appropriately. He is able to spell a range of words accurately, including less regular words, for example *cement* and *buffalo*. His two spelling errors are plausible. His use of *roves* for roofs shows that he is familiar with irregular forms of pluralisation in particular from -f (singular) to -ves (plural) as in hoof–hooves, but has not represented the long 'oo' phoneme in the middle of the word. His use of *to* where *too* is needed in the phrase *too hot* is a common one, as is the use of *there* where *they're* is needed in the sentence *They're made from buffalo skin.*

Michael's handwriting is joined, fluent and easy to read. He joins all letters in a consistent style. His representation of letters is generally accurate although the challenge of writing on unlined paper may have made it harder for him to maintain consistent size differences – for example keeping capital letters and ascenders, (eg, in f, l, k) taller than other letters.

Summary of Michael's writing development

As we can see in the samples of writing above, Michael has made great progress in his mastery of writing. In Sample 1 his meaning is communicated through drawing, a string of random letter shapes, and his shared communication with a supportive adult. At this early stage of writing, young children often represent meanings significant to them through drawing, or combining drawings with such letter-like forms, and by talking about their representations. This is an important stage in writing for the child as they begin to make the links between their own lives, and ways of expressing themselves through talk and gesture, to drawing and writing.

In Samples 2, 3 and 4, we can see how Michael is becoming increasingly confident in making his meaning clear in written language, and he supports this with well-selected and relevant illustrations. What is also notable is Michael's increasing mastery of the conventions of spelling, grammar and punctuation. We can see how his knowledge of how texts are organised has grown. He is aware of the different kinds of information and messages that he can convey to the reader. Unlike the early writing in Sample 1, Michael's meaning is now clearly communicated to the reader without an explanation from him. In Samples 3 and 4 he is able to choose relevant information and present this by choosing words and phrases and organising text and images in order to communicate meaning with increasing precision and clarity.

Teaching grammar

Developing children's understanding of specific language features and the ways in which they can be used can be described as a 'contextualised' approach to the teaching of grammar, whereby children learn about grammatical features in the context of their reading and writing. For instance, in the Year 3 classroom, in order to support her class in using persuasive language in their brochures, Chris brought in a range of published materials used to advertise and provide information about tourist attractions. The children worked together to identify where adjectives and superlatives had been used and discussed their impact on the reader. Using this knowledge, the class then discussed and planned how adjectives and superlatives could be used most effectively in their own brochures.

Research focus

Research into the teaching of grammar

Myhill, D (2011) *Harnessing Grammar: Weaving Words and Shaping Texts.* York: Institute for Effective Education (IEE), University of York. Available at www. betterevidence.files.wordpress.com/2011/03/better_language_arts_sample_ article.pdf.

Debra Myhill is an educationalist with extensive experience of research into the effective teaching of language and literacy, particularly writing. Her recent research has highlighted the importance of teaching grammar through meaningful language contexts, where language choices can be discussed and explored in terms of their impact on meaning. Explicit understanding of language then becomes a tool for creativity in language use. Children are taught terminology to enhance this process rather than as an end in itself. Although this research was conducted in secondary classrooms, its findings are very relevant to primary teachers.

You can watch an interview with Debra Myhill at www.youtube.com/ watch?v=VXr09X86K20.

The teaching of grammar within the primary curriculum has seen considerable change over recent years. In England, the introduction of the Spelling, Grammar and Punctuation (SPaG) test for children completing their primary education in 2013 and the draft 2014 national curriculum (DfE, 2013) has raised the profile of the teaching of grammar. The statutory requirements include lists of specific grammatical terms to be covered over the primary years. The SPaG test assesses understanding through a series of multiple choice and short-answer questions, focusing on children's ability to understand terms – eg, 'adverb', 'connective', 'subordinate clauses' – and to complete exercises related to isolated sentences. A key challenge for primary teachers is therefore to find ways to engage children in understanding the way language works, equipping them with the relevant terms to enable them to explore, analyse and use language effectively, as well as to perform successfully in this type of formal assessment. For a teacher of primary English a thorough understanding of how language works and relevant grammatical terminology is therefore essential. If this is not an area in which you feel confident it would be useful to begin to revise and develop your knowledge by pursuing the suggestions for 'taking it further' shown in the following section.

PREPARING FOR TEACHING PRIMARY ENGLISH

Reflective task

Look back at the examples used in this chapter.

o   Consider the teaching of speaking and listening in each classroom. How are the children given a purpose and audience for their talk?

o   How do the demands on children's speaking and listening skills grow as children become more mature language users?

o   Consider the teaching of reading in each classroom. How are the children motivated to read and encouraged to enjoy literature?

o   How do the demands on children's reading skills grow as children become more confident and competent in their reading?

o   Consider the teaching of writing in each classroom. How are the children motivated to write?

o   How do the demands on children's writing skills grow as children become more confident and competent in their writing?

o   Consider how the activities described link speaking and listening, reading and writing.

As you can see, English in the primary curriculum is a broad and complex subject. If you decide to become a primary teacher, you will need to draw on extensive and secure knowledge about language. You may never have studied language or gained an explicit understanding of how it functions, but this has not prevented you from developing the ability to communicate effectively. However, as a primary classroom teacher, responsible for children's development in language and literacy, you will need a more conscious understanding of how language works. Such explicit knowledge about language will underpin your ability to plan appropriate activities, select resources, and support and assess children's progress in all aspects of English. It will also enable you to be clear and precise about aspects of language you teach and provide a classroom environment that will foster interest, creativity and enthusiasm for language use.

Learning about language, literacy and its development will continue throughout your career. During your teacher preparation course you will further your understanding of classroom practice, the theory underpinning this and children's development as language

Table 5.1 Reviewing your knowledge

Key areas	Purpose/relevance to teaching Such knowledge will enable you to...	Aspects and examples
Knowledge about children's literature	Encourage children's enjoyment of reading; foster their development as independent readers; find personal favourites for sharing with children and using them as a focus for classroom activities	Reading a wide range of children's literature – picture books, novels and poetry by a wide range of authors
Knowledge about texts	Select appropriate texts to use as models in the classroom; make features explicit to children; support their progress in producing them	Digital texts – features of screen-based texts; range of types of text Genres (types of text) of fiction – adventure, fantasy, science fiction, etc. – and their features Genres of non-fiction – report, persuasion, recount, etc. – and their features
Knowledge about vocabulary, spelling and phonology	Develop children's interest in language and their understanding of the ways in which letters are combined and their significance for reading and writing (in particular in relation to phonics and spelling)	Confidence in the accuracy of your own spelling and/or your ability to deal with challenges in spelling Awareness of morphology – the formation of words through the combination of parts, eg, prefixes and suffixes Awareness of word origins – varied languages that have provided English vocabulary Understanding of phonology – the way in which sounds are represented by specific letters and combinations and the relevant terminology used to identify these (eg, phoneme, grapheme, digraph, trigraph, etc.) as used in phonics teaching
Knowledge about grammar and punctuation; explicit knowledge about language features	Be clear and specific in guiding children's language use, assessing their progress and recognising useful texts as models for the classroom	Key terms for word classes (eg, nouns, verbs, adverbs, adjectives, pronouns) and the ability to identify these and recognise their function in texts Clause/phrase/sentence and sentence types Forms of punctuation and their functions Cohesion – ways of joining parts of a text or sentence Standard English Active/passive voice

and literacy users. In the meantime, in preparing your application for initial teacher prepa-ration, use Table 5.1 to help you review what you know and identify your needs for revision or development. This table lists key aspects of knowledge about language and literacy that you are likely to need, with some examples, along with an indication of why they are impor-tant. Suggested sources of support for each area are listed underneath the table.

CONCLUSION

As we hope you will have seen from this chapter, English is an exciting and rewarding subject to teach. Its scope is broad, varied and, as language continues to evolve and its use expands with technological developments, it is also ever-changing. Through this subject, children are equipped with essential skills needed in order to learn and suc-ceed across the curriculum as well as in the world outside the classroom. They also gain enthusiasm and confidence as users of language and literacy, which will extend well beyond their years in school. English is therefore an area of considerable responsibility for a teacher but also presents plenty of rewards and exciting opportunities for engaging children in motivating and meaningful activities.

At this initial stage of applying for teacher preparation, the scope and demands of the subject can be daunting, but we hope that this chapter has enabled you to see how you can begin to prepare yourself for what is involved. The first step is to ensure that you are well-equipped and confident in your subject knowledge and we hope that this chapter will help you to begin to consider how to approach this, as well as to see the exciting opportunities ahead.

 Progress checklist

- Use Table 5.1 to review your own knowledge about language and literacy. Identify and address any aspects for development.

- Find opportunities to talk to children about their interests and use of literacy within the classroom and at home.

- Visit classrooms and observe and talk to teachers in order to find out about how they encourage children to become enthusiastic and confident users of language and literacy, and the activities they use to enable children to progress in speaking and listening, reading and writing. Observe phonics teaching in a number of age phases and note how this supports children's reading and writing.

- Find out about the new statutory requirements for teaching English in the national curriculum from 2014.

- Develop a list/database/collection of favourite books that you can look forward to sharing with children.

JARGON BUSTER

Dialects: different regional varieties of a particular language. These include differences in vocabulary and grammar. 'Accent' refers more specifically to the pronunciation of a language by a particular group of language users.

Graphemes: letters and letter combinations that represent phonemes, or sounds in language. For example, the word 'rain' has three phonemes (or sounds), which are represented by three graphemes: 'r-ai-n'.

Home language: this is the first language, or native language, that a child learned from birth, or at the critical period of learning to speak.

Phonemes: the smallest units of sound that make up a language. There are approximately 44 in the English language, dependent on variation in regional accents.

Phonemic awareness: the ability to hear the sounds in language and manipulate these.

Specific language features: use of aspects of language to create meaning and impact. For example, in conversation, describing an embarrassing experience, we may use hyperbole – ie, exaggeration – to make the incident more amusing for our audience. Similes and metaphors – comparisons of one item with another – are often used to make the meaning clearer or more vivid, eg, 'Life is like a box of chocolates; you never know what you're going to get' highlights the uncertainty of life but in a light-hearted way. Individual words are also chosen for effect; for example, the use of the adjective 'essential' to describe 'skills' in the third sentence of this chapter highlights their importance.

Standard English: *a variety (or dialect) of English distinguished from other dialects by its use of grammar and vocabulary and its status, as it is the form of English used in official and formal contexts. Key differences with regional dialects include:*

○ *the irregular past tense for the verb to be: I <u>was</u>, you/we/they <u>were</u>, s/he it <u>was</u> (whereas some regional dialects use I <u>were</u>, you/we/they were, s/he it <u>were</u>);*

○ *the irregular present tense for the verb to do: I <u>do</u>, you/we/they <u>do</u>, s/he it does (whereas some regional dialects use I <u>does</u>, you/we/they <u>does</u>, s/he it does);*

○ *irregular formation of reflexive pronouns, himself, themselves (whereas some regional dialects use hisself and theirselves);*

○ *the single use of a negative: I don't want any; I haven't been to a... (whereas some regional dialects use I don't want no...; I ain't been to no..., etc.);*

○ *lack of distinction between you (singular) and you (plural) (whereas some regional dialects use thou (singular) and you/youse (plural)).*

Systematic synthetic phonics: *this is an approach to teaching phonics that works on the principle of breaking words down into their constituent phonemes, or sounds in the early stages of reading. Children are taught to read by synthesising (or blending) the phonemes in the order that they occur in the word. They are taught to spell by segmenting (or splitting) words into sounds, and then writing the corresponding graphemes. The grapheme–phoneme correspondences (match between graphemes and their corresponding sounds) are taught in a systematic and incremental sequence.*

▶▶ **TAKING IT FURTHER**

Cremin, T (2009) *Teaching English Creatively*. London: Routledge.

Crystal, D (1990) *Rediscover Grammar*. London: Longman.

Eyres, I (2007) *English for Primary and Early Years: Developing Subject Knowledge*. London: Sage/Open University.

Medwell, J, Moore, G, Wray, D and Griffiths, V (2011) *Primary English Knowledge and Understanding*, 5th edition. Exeter: Learning Matters.

Riley, J (2006) *Language and Literacy 3–7: Creative Approaches to Teaching*. London: Sage.

Whitehead, M (2007) *Developing Language and Literacy with Young Children*, 3rd edition. London: Paul Chapman Publishing.

Wilson, A and Scanlon, J (2011) *Language Knowledge for Primary Teachers*. London: David Fulton Publishers.

These titles recommend a creative approach to English teaching and focus on teaching approaches for speaking and listening, reading and writing that draw upon and support children's capacity to be creative.

Glazzard, J and Stokoe, J. (2013) *Teaching Systematic Synthetic Phonics and Early English*. Northwich: Critical Publishing.

Provides an overview of systematic synthetic phonics and other aspects of early English provision.

www.cybergrammar.co.uk

A site designed to support and develop knowledge of grammar and to indicate its relevance in the classroom.

www.justimaginestorycentre.co.uk

www.lovereading4kids.co.uk

www.readingzone.com/home.php

These sites are for use by children, teachers and parents to find out about children's literature, authors and ways of using books in the classroom.

REFERENCES

Cremin, T, Mottram, M, Collins, F, Powell, S and Safford, K (2009) Teachers as Readers: Building Communities of Readers. *Literacy*, 43(1): 11–19.

Department for Education (DfE) (2013) *The National Curriculum in England: Framework Document for Consultation*. London: Crown Publications. Available at www.media. education.gov.uk/assets/files/pdf/n/national%20curriculum%20consultation%20 -%20framework%20document.pdf.

Dombey, H (2010) *Teaching Reading: What the Evidence Says*. Leicester: United Kingdom Literacy Association.

Inkpen, M (1992) *Kipper's Toybox*. London: Hodder Children's Books.

Rose, J (2006) *Independent Review of the Teaching of Early Reading*. Nottingham: DfES Publications.

Sachar, L (1998) *Holes*. New York: Yearling.

6 Developing subject knowledge in mathematics

Adrian Fearn

INTRODUCTION

When discussing mathematical subject knowledge with student teachers and staff in school, there is often an implicit understanding that 'it' is very important. Mathematical subject knowledge is also required by the Teachers' Standards (DfE 2012a). In England, this focus on subject knowledge in maths was evident through the Williams Review (2008), whereby Sir Peter Williams was asked by the government of the time to undertake an independent review of maths teaching in early years settings and primary schools. One of the six areas that the secretary of state asked Sir Peter to look at was:

What conceptual and subject knowledge of mathematics should be expected of primary school teachers and early years practitioners, and how should Initial Teacher Training (ITT) and continuing professional development (CPD) be improved to secure that knowledge.

(Williams, 2008, p 2)

Through visits to schools and the involvement of more than 200,000 teachers and wider practitioners he concluded that:

Confidence and dexterity in the classroom are essential prerequisites for the successful teacher of mathematics and children are perhaps the most acutely sensitive barometer of any uncertainty on their part. The review believes that this confidence stems from deep mathematical subject and pedagogical knowledge and it has therefore examined the available provision in mathematics during Initial Teacher Training (ITT) and education.

(Williams, 2008, p 3)

His words here inform the structure of this chapter. First, the chapter looks at why confidence and attitude are so important in maths teaching. It then moves on to focus on 'deep mathematical subject and pedagogical knowledge'. Don't worry for now what these terms mean, but clearly they are important for you as someone who is considering applying for an initial teacher preparation programme. What is also clear is that the focus on mathematical subject knowledge is nothing new and this will continue to be high on the agenda of teacher educators. For example, the Cockcroft Report of 1982 (Cockcroft, 1982) focused on the often unconscious messages that teachers give off around maths, while one of the key recommendations of the recent Ofsted *Made to Measure* report (2012) was to *promote enhancement of subject knowledge and subject-specific teaching skills in all routes through primary initial teacher education* (Ofsted, 2012, p 9). Clearly then, subject knowledge in maths matters, so we will begin by looking at yours and how it has been shaped by a variety of factors.

ATTITUDE AND CONFIDENCE – THEY MATTER!

This first area of subject knowledge to be looked at is your mathematical disposition.

Reflective task

○ Reflect on your interactions with maths from birth to the present day. There may have been key moments and people along the way – what have been the highs and lows?

○ As you think about your journey, draw this on a graph like the one in Figure 6.1 below.

○ Where your graph peaks either side of the horizontal line, think about the following questions:

○ Why did you feel like this?

Positive

Birth   Now

Negative

Figure 6.1 Key maths moments

○ Was this specific to maths or did you feel this in other subjects too?

○ If you were a teacher what could you have done to help?

○ How do you feel about teaching maths to children?

The last question will have been shaped by all sorts of factors, some of which are probably below the line on the graph. For example, did you have a particular teacher that made maths very 'high-stakes' through tables tests? Were the results of these tests made public to the rest of the class? I still feel very uncomfortable when I see 'class times tables progress charts' in classrooms where children's names are next to the tables they are working on. How might the child feel who has short-term memory problems and never moves off the two times table? Why does it matter to anyone else what table a child is working on? Why do we compare one child to the rest of the class?

Do you also have moments above the line? Often these may be associated with something you have achieved and worked hard for, such as passing your GCSE maths or achieving a certain level in a test, such as Key Stage 2 SATs (Standardised Assessment Tasks). You may want to think back again now and see if you can add anything else to the graph. For example, was there a particular teacher who made maths fun and enjoyable, or a particular day or week when you were undertaking some maths that you really enjoyed?

Hopefully, you will see from undertaking the reflective task how your attitude has been shaped by your experiences. Linked into your attitude is how you see your ability in maths and whether maths as a subject is 'different'. Complete the reflective task below and see whether your views change in any way.

Reflective task

Consider the following statement:

Maths is something you're either good at or you're not

Agree —————————— Not sure —————————— Disagree

(You've got a maths   (Need to find out   (It's something you
gene or not)   more)   work at)

o   Try to place yourself on the line above depending on how you feel about the
    statement.

How did you get on with the second part of the task? Wherever you put yourself it is absolutely fine, but you may want to consider the implications for children who struggle with maths if they do not believe that they can ever succeed as they do not have the ability. Try sharing the graph and question above with family and friends and compare responses.

An American researcher, Carol Dweck, explored girls' beliefs about mathematics. She concluded that:

some views can harm people by telling them – in advance – that they don't have the skills … public dialogue and the scientific inquiry are best directed, not at deciding who has math and science ability and who does not, but rather at how best to foster those abilities.

(Dweck, 2006, p 12)

While there may be some people who find the subject more challenging than others, teachers need to 'foster' the ability that every individual has to the maximum, irrespective of their current level of attainment. Zoe Rhydderch-Evans (2002) echoes the work of

Guy Claxton (whose work is explored in Chapter 8) when she outlines the three qualities that *constitute a good learning temperament* for the mathematical learner:

○   resilience and persistence;

○   a playful disposition;

○   conviviality.

Resilience and persistence

The first bullet point suggests that we need children to understand that sometimes learning is hard and that for maths it is not always about a page of ticks. Often a problem has to be grappled with and sometimes it is very challenging. For this approach to work, there needs to be a supportive classroom environment where effort is celebrated, not who is on what page of the textbook or how many maths exercise books a year you have got through with pages of very similar calculations! Have a go at the magic triangles activity below to gauge your own resilience. As with all the activities included in the chapter, answers are provided at the end.

Reflective task

Have a go at this activity and see how long you give yourself before you give up. How persistent are you? Do you come back to the problem later? Did you enjoy the challenge? Did you look at the answers at the end of the chapter to check or through frustration? The activity is often called magic triangles. You may want to reflect on whether any magic is involved.

○   Using the numbers 1–6, place them in a 3×3 triangle as shown below. Can you organise them in different ways so that the total of every side comes to 9, 10, 11 and finally 12?

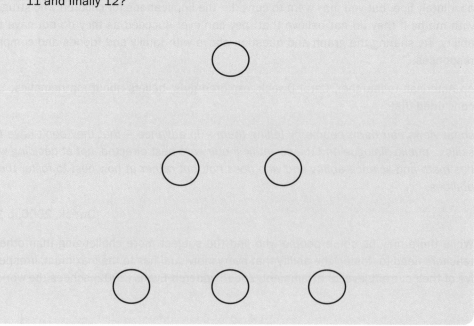

A playful disposition

A playful disposition is also important for good learning. This could be at many different levels, but there is an underlying assumption that play is a very good vehicle for learning. This could be playing with numbers to solve a problem such as the one above or playing a maths games with peers. Put simply, this is about encouraging a 'have a go' attitude, and celebrating both effort and the final answer (if there is one). A great starter in a maths lesson is to write up a number as an answer and see if the class can challenge themselves to come up with possible questions. Of course the list is infinite, which itself is a tricky concept!

Conviviality

The final aspect of Rhydderch-Evans' (2002) mathematical attitude is that of conviviality, which means enjoying the learning with friends. To look at what this means for maths, undertake the following reflective task, which concerns you as a maths learner.

Reflective task

Try to take yourself back to your years in junior school and draw yourself in a maths lesson.

The drawing you have made may be like many of the ones that the children did during a study by Borthwick (2011), with maths seen as a very solitary experience. Your drawing may have you sitting at a desk looking at the teacher, which is in line with the findings of Ofsted, who found that, *A feature of much of the satisfactory teaching was that teachers tended to talk for too long* (Ofsted, 2012, p 26).

Having opened this chapter by looking at attitude to maths teaching and learning, the next task is designed to enable you to summarise what you have learned so far and how this has influenced the sort of a maths teacher you want to be.

Reflective task

○ Why is attitude towards maths important?

○ Has your answer to this question changed as you have read the chapter so far?

○ What sort of maths teacher do you want to be?

Attitude alone is not enough

Of course, attitude alone is not enough. The rest of this chapter looks at other aspects of subject knowledge that teachers need in order to be effective teachers of maths. These

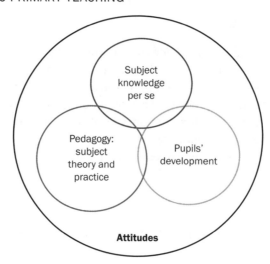

Figure 6.2 Aspects of subject knowledge (Shulman, 1986)

are usually accredited to Lee Shulman (1986) and shown as a Venn Diagram, as can be seen in Figure 6.2.

As you can see, attitude surrounds the three elements of the Venn diagram, a clear indication of its importance, and the reason why this chapter opened by looking at your attitude towards maths. The three other elements all interplay to make an effective maths teacher, which is hopefully what you aspire to be. So, let us unpick these three areas to see their differing roles and set targets for you to develop your skills on your journey towards applying for a course of initial teacher preparation.

'Subject knowledge per se' is sometimes also referred to as 'subject matter knowledge' and is something that you will already have lots of, but just may not have used for some time. It encompasses your body of mathematical knowledge, such as the properties of an equilateral triangle or knowing how to add one-fifth to three-eighths. You may also find here that you have mathematical knowledge that you actually have no understanding of. For example, why do two minuses make a plus? This section of the chapter helps you audit your current level of knowledge and makes you examine some of the maths that you may have learnt, but in a deeper way, so that you hopefully actually understand it, which is crucial if you are trying to teach it to someone else.

With 'pupils' development', subject knowledge is concerned with the teacher understanding the progression of mathematical learning. If a child is finding something difficult, do you know how to support them with prior learning? Conversely, if a child clearly already understands what you are trying to teach them, do you know where to take them next? To support you in this, later in the chapter the relevant curriculum documents will be examined and scenarios given for you to reflect upon.

'Pedagogy: subject theory and practice' is often the term that seems the most daunting, but need not be. Put simply, it is the choice you make about how you teach. In maths, this often involves the use of resources, for example a 100 square or a blank number line to teach an aspect of number such as adding ten. A skilled teacher here will have a broad repertoire of strategies and may have a bank of resources to use, based on experience. At the moment, your experience may only be from the viewpoint of a learner having maths 'done' to them. We will therefore examine the choices that teachers have and how these impact on the learner.

> ## Reflective task
>
> Think back to your key moments graph that you drew at the start of the chapter. If there are some key individual teachers on there, reflect on how their strengths as a maths teacher, or not, relate to the three subject knowledge areas shown in Figure 6.2. For example, when you were struggling with a concept did the teacher leave you to grapple on alone or support you by taking you back a step, showing good curriculum subject knowledge?

No chapter on subject knowledge could hope to provide you with everything you need. However, the rest of the chapter will guide you in beginning your journey to gaining a place on a course of teacher preparation, through helping you to reflect on what you already know and setting clear targets for your next steps in developing your mathematical subject knowledge in the three areas highlighted above.

SUBJECT KNOWLEDGE PER SE

As discussed, this area of subject knowledge is concerned with you as a prospective teacher understanding the mathematical body of knowledge yourself in order to be able to teach others. When discussing this area of subject knowledge with new student teachers many still have a poor attitude to maths and quite happily profess that they cannot do maths, even though they have been highly successful in their mathematical development as they achieved a grade C or above at GCSE. When discussing this further, many suggest that they achieved this without much understanding and just followed procedures that gained marks. Such reflection on their learning prompts them to ask some fairly fundamental questions such as, what do we mean by 'understanding'? Try the reflective task below, which focuses on your mathematical understanding.

> ## Reflective task
>
> Look at the series of statements below, some of which are true and some of which are false. For each:
>
> o   state whether it is true or false;
>
> o   reflect on whether you understand it;
>
> o   see if you can explain it to someone else so that they understand it.
>
> Two minuses make a plus.

Multiplying always makes numbers bigger.

A square is also a rectangle.

If the decimal in a number is 0.1 to 0.5, you always round up.

Once you have thought these through, look at the end of this chapter for the answers and some guidance around the subject knowledge underpinning them. If you want some more of these to fox your friends with, there is a very thorough list, with discussion, on the Count On website, www.counton.org/resources/misconceptions.

Auditing your own subject knowledge

Earlier in this chapter you undertook some reflection around your attitude towards maths. The chapter is now concerned with you auditing your own understanding of maths, to see what you know and then need to work on. Either during or after you have attempted these, it is really important that you reflect on your maths and set yourself some very clear targets using Table 6.1 at the end of this section. If you haven't already passed the qualified teacher status (QTS) skills tests, this activity will give you some useful feedback to work on.

Reflective task

1. Complete the table below filling in the gaps.

Fraction	Percentage	Decimal
	50%	
		0.125
	75%	
$\frac{3}{8}$		
$\frac{1}{10}$		
	150%	
$\frac{1}{4}$		

2. Put these fractions and decimals in order from smallest to largest (no calculator allowed).

    $\frac{3}{4}$ $\frac{2}{5}$ 0.3   0.07 $\frac{1}{10}$ 0.125 $\frac{1}{2}$

3. In a class of 32 children, the ratio of children having free school meals to children not having free school meals is 1:3. How many children do not have free school meals?

4. I think of a number and add 3. I then half it and multiply by 4. My answer is 16. What number did I think of?

5. Divide 0.3 by 100.

6. Sheila works in a café where baked potatoes are a speciality, the most popular filling for which is cottage cheese. Each potato uses three-fifths of a tub of cottage cheese. Sheila has 4 tubs of cottage cheese in the fridge. How many portions can she serve? (Adapted from a problem in Cohen, 2004.)

Table 6.1 Personal action plan

Area of maths	Red, Amber, Green (RAG) rating Red – really struggled/no idea why answer is wrong Amber – got there but had to work at it Green – confident in this area	Action
Fractions and decimals	Red	Seek support on making them all a decimal so I can compare

Another really good source of questions to work through are past Year 6 SATs papers. These are all available online, and are often published on school websites. The following link has many maths questions grouped by learning objective and would make a good starting point: www.edu.dudley.gov.uk/numeracy/mj/slnmdec10/pri_ma_frmwrk_y6_pitchexpect.pdf.

If you want to try some more tasks to enhance your subject knowledge, this website has a really thorough audit to try: www.cimt.plymouth.ac.uk/interactive/mat/default.htm.

Reviewing your subject knowledge

Having engaged with some maths you now need to identify what you need to do to address the areas in which you do not feel confident and set yourself some targets. Target-setting will be an important process during your initial teacher preparation, so being aware of what you need to work on and being able to work out what you need to do to address this is a good skill to develop. After the maths you have undertaken so far, fill in a table like Table 6.1 to develop a 'personal action plan' based on a traffic lights red, amber or green system. An example is given, which might be relevant to you if you found question 2, above, hard.

Table 6.2 Expectations for children's use of language related to shape (for children aged 5 and 11)

Area of shape, space or measure	Associated vocabulary	
	5 years old	11 years old (new words from the left column)
Measures of size/length/distance		
Time		
2D shape		

PUPILS' DEVELOPMENT

We now move on to look at another important aspect of subject knowledge, that of understanding pupils' mathematical development. It would be impossible to look at the development of every strand of maths within this chapter, but we can examine why it is important to know about this and look closely at a few examples to set your thinking and subject knowledge development on its way. We start by going back to the early years of a child's development and looking at the use of language.

If you have a much younger sibling or child of your own, you may find the following task easier. At the end of the Foundation Stage in England, at age five, there are two Early Learning Goals (ELGs) for maths, one for 'number' and one for 'shape, space and measure'. The ELG for shape, space and measure suggests that children have to use 'everyday language' for these different aspects expected of a five-year-old.

Reflective task

Complete Table 6.2 by asking yourself what would be expected learning and associated language for different aspects of shape at age five, and then at age 11. For example would you expect a five-year-old to say that a shape is 'congruent'? You might then want to consider the steps in between.

Documenting progression

Now that you have had a chance to reflect on your own understanding of progression, look at how it is set out in statutory frameworks. Normally, in England, the progression for any subject is laid out in the first instance in the form of a national curriculum. At the time of writing in 2013, there is an existing national curriculum from 2000 and a new one that will become statutory from 2014. These are:

o   National curriculum from 2000 (DfEE, 1999): www.educationengland. org.uk/documents/pdfs/1999-nc-primary-handbook.pdf;

o   National Curriculum from 2014 (DfE, 2013): www.media.education.gov.uk/assets/ files/pdf/m/mathematics%20-%20key%20stages%201%20and%202.pdf.

Both are useful documents to read to begin to see the mathematical journey that children take as they move through primary school, through Key Stage 1 and into Key Stage 2. In terms of subject knowledge, the phrases that you will commonly hear about the children you teach, whatever age, is that you need to understand *what has gone before* and *what they need next*. A good analogy to use, that you may be able to empathise with, is that of learning to drive. For example, did you immediately start with a hill start or reversing round a bend on your first lesson? Of course not – you built up small skills along the way. Did you ever have to go back over a skill that you thought you had mastered but then needed more practice? This is the skill that a qualified teacher will have developed – the ability to know when the pitch of learning is right for a child to make progress. However, to do that you need to understand progression within your subject.

For the calculation aspect of number, schools will often have a calculation policy that shows how this progresses throughout school. Try the reflective task below to develop your understanding of progression in calculation. You may remember being taught many of these methods at school if you were in England from around 1998. Many of these strategies and methods were laid out in the National Numeracy Strategy, which included an outline of expected progression in maths for all pupils from Reception to Year 6 (DfES, 2006).

Reflective task

Use an internet search engine to search for 'school calculation policy'. You will find a good list of schools' policies to choose from. Alternatively, if you are undertaking some voluntary work in a school, you could ask the maths subject leader if they could spend some time showing you their policy. Once you have a policy, choose one aspect of calculation to see how this progresses through the school. An interesting strand to choose is that of division, as this involves a method called 'chunking', which seems to evoke strong opinions as to whether it is a useful method or not. Reflect on whether any methods are new to you and how they build from more informal methods, such as using number lines, into more formal written methods of calculation.

If you decide to be a teacher, one of the most powerful ways of developing your knowledge of pupils' development is by teaching different year groups. Any course of teacher preparation will place a strong emphasis on having opportunities to teach in different year groups and Key Stages. However, for now, try to spend time in school working with children of different age groups. Even if you are dead-set that you only want to teach Years 5 or 6, you still need to spend time in the early years and Key Stage 1 to see how a child's mathematical journey progresses and begin to develop your knowledge of children's mathematical development.

PEDAGOGY: SUBJECT THEORY AND PRACTICE

This aspect of subject knowledge is often referred to as pedagogical content knowledge, abbreviated to PCK (Shulman, 1986). This may sound a very daunting term, as

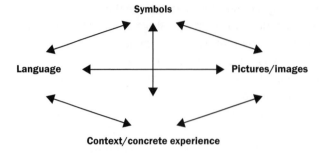

Figure 6.3 Making connections (Haylock and Cockburn, 2013, used with kind permission)

discussed earlier, but essentially relates to the choices you make about how you teach maths to children. Derek Haylock and Anne Cockburn, whose books are in the 'taking it further' section at the end of this chapter, use a simple diagram to outline how children learn maths through making connections (see Figure 6.3). The diagram suggests that when learning an aspect of maths there are four key elements that interact. These are:

○ context/concrete experience: these are physical objects, such as counters, toys, fingers, dice – essentially anything that you can touch;

○ language: this can be specific mathematical language, such as 'triangle' or more general 'how many?' forms of language. Some words, 'take away' or 'table', for example, can have multiple meanings;

○ pictures/images: this may be something that you draw on, like a number line or diagrams that involve sorting or matching by a certain criteria;

○ symbols: +, =, £, %, 4 and so on.

To understand the diagram, consider each of the four elements above and relate them to an area of maths teaching, as in the reflective task below. For example, if a young child was playing a domino game, they would connect the number of dots as the picture/image with the number word for that arrangement of dots. The context here would be a game. Later, they may begin to connect with a numerical symbol from their experience of say, a birthday card. Figure 6.4 illustrates this for the number six. Decisions a teacher makes about what to use and how to use it are an important part of PCK, although not the only element.

Reflective task

Use the four interrelated elements of Haylock and Cockburn's model to consider how you might introduce the concept of division. Would you use any pictures or images? Would the children have anything physical to use as a concrete experience? Would you use different language depending on the age of the children? Would you straight away expect the children to make sense of the division symbol or other symbols we use for division?

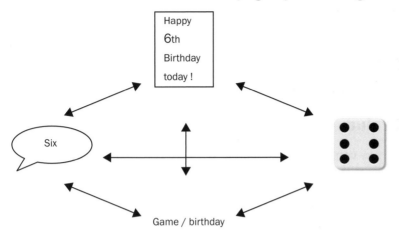

Figure 6.4 Connecting 6

As you consider this reflective task, you might start remembering some maths 'equipment' that you used at school, such as place value cards. These are often referred to in the United Kingdom as 'models and images' and in the United States and other countries as 'manipulatives'. Without getting into the slight differences between the terms, they are essentially maths 'stuff' and an essential part of the toolkit that a skilled maths teacher uses as part of their pedagogy, or choice of teaching approach.

Reflective task

Think about the mathematical 'stuff' you remember from your own schooling or have seen used in school and make a list of it. Do not worry if you don't know the name of the model or image – just draw it. If you can, think about whether you found these models and images helpful or not.

CHILDREN'S COMMON MISCONCEPTIONS

Let us consider now a final skill, that of dealing with children's misconceptions. Some of these misconceptions have been touched on earlier, such as that multiplying a number always makes it bigger, but let us unpick a few more to develop your ability to understand what goes beneath the answer a child gives a teacher, so that you can support a child in dealing with the misconception. There are some excellent books on this subject, which are referenced at the end of this chapter in 'taking it further', but the following scenarios illustrate a few of the very common misconceptions and what a skilled teacher might do to help the child.

Scenario 1

Money and value

Money is a very tricky context for children. Put out a 2p coin and a 5p coin and ask a child, *Which is bigger?* Many children will say the 2p and be absolutely correct as it feels physically bigger to hold and looks bigger. Even if you ask the question differently such as *Which of these coins would you rather have to buy sweets with?*, many children will still ask for the 2p due to its size. Money relies on the concept of value and all of the UK accepting that a blue/green piece of paper with pictures of the queen on is worth £5.

Scenario 2

Money and equivalence

Put out 100 × 1p coins and 1 × £1 coin. Are they the same? Well, yes and no. They have the same value as discussed in the scenario above but they are not physically the same. However, in terms of value they are the same. In terms of pedagogy here it is useful to talk to children about why it might not be a good idea to have to carry around 100 1p pieces. They very quickly get the idea of equivalence and exchange.

CONCLUSION

This chapter has encouraged you to reflect on all aspects of mathematical subject knowledge, from your own attitude towards maths, through to which mathematical resources to use to support children's learning. Through engaging with the reflective tasks in the chapter you will have developed your own level of subject knowledge and be able to talk fluently about the different aspects.

Finally, as a member of society, it is important to look beyond your own mathematical knowledge into the implications for society of poor maths skills. A fascinating study undertaken by the Every Child a Chance Trust and KPMG (2008) highlights the cost of not getting it right at school and beyond. Their key findings are summarised below and make quite startling reading.

For women, poor numeracy was an independent predictor of:

o   poor physical health;

o   depression;

o   a belief that they lacked control over their lives;

o   the probability of being out of the labour market (regardless of how many children they had);

o   or, if in work, of being in an unskilled or semi-skilled job;

o   the probability of living in a household where no one works.

For men, poor numeracy, even when their literacy was good, indicated:

o   that they were less likely to be in a company pension scheme;

o   increased risk of depression;

o   increased probability of having been suspended from school, or arrested and cautioned by the police.

Hopefully, these statistics show clearly that as a prospective teacher your role in engaging children with maths is vital for their long-term development and wellbeing.

Answers and comments for reflective tasks

Magic triangles (page 94)

Solution 1

Solution 3

Solution 4

Two minuses make a plus (page 97)

There is an interesting thread on a website called The Student Room where, after four or five individuals have tried to explain this, eventually someone comes in with *Don't question it, just accept it*, which is exactly the problem here with how many of us have been taught.

To unpick this you first need to understand that the minuses do different things. Have a look at the number sentence and the number line below. Note here that it is not called a sum because that is an addition word and just adds to the confusion.

$$5 - -5 = 10$$

−5   0   +5

In the number sentence, the first minus is actually the operation of subtraction. The second minus, which is next to the 5, makes the 5 a minus or negative 5. Within subtraction there are two types: take away and difference. Imagine the number line above being one for temperature. Clearly we do not physically take away any temperature, so the operation is the difference between the two numbers. How many numbers are there between minus 5 and plus 5? 10! The basic problem here is that one minus is an operation and the other stays with the number to make it a negative. The subject knowledge here raises many questions around the teaching of negative numbers and whether difference has been taught as a form of subtraction. Both are hot topics, and something that you should address through your initial teacher preparation.

Multiplying always makes numbers bigger (page 98)

What is $\frac{1}{2} \times 8$?

The answer is 4, but this may seem very odd as the 8 has got smaller. To understand this you need to attach a different meaning to $\frac{1}{2}$ times 8 in order to unpick what is happening. Try replacing the word 'times' with 'of'. So, the above is half of 8, which is 4. This works for whole-number multiplication too, it just makes you think about multiplication differently. For example, if you have two boxes 'of' six eggs, you would write 2×6.

A square is also a rectangle (page 98)

At last, a misconception that is not to do with numbers, although the number four is crucial here, as you will see. This one is all to do with definitions.

A square is commonly defined as, *A plane figure with four equal straight sides and four right angles*. A rectangle is *A four-sided flat shape with straight sides where all interior angles are right angles (90°)*.

If you apply the properties, a square works for both, thus making a square a particular type of rectangle, ie, one with all the sides the same length. A square is also a type of rhombus. So, when teaching shape you need to make sure that your understanding of definitions is correct, but this also raises questions around how shape is taught and progression. If 2D shape is only ever taught by looking at the physical shape on paper then when you come to apply the definitions, this may cause confusion as you have a very fixed image of what the shape is and its name, whereas it may have a number of names. A maths dictionary makes a very useful subject knowledge resource to ensure you are clear about the properties of shape. A useful online version is www.mathsisfun.com/quadrilaterals.html.

If the decimal in a number is 0.1 to 0.5, you always round up (page 98)

I'm sure that like me you have been taught the 'rule' for rounding numbers, so 6.3 is rounded to 6.0 and 6.7 would be rounded to 7.0. Have a go at the question below and see how your rounding rule works.

○   244 children and 24 adults from Stoney Field School go on a coach trip. How many 38-seat coaches does the school need to hire?

If you used a calculator you may have added 244 to 24 to get 268 and divided this by 38 to give you 7.052... So, if you apply the rounding rule, you round down to 7 and have 7 buses that carry 38 people, giving space for 266. Oh, dear there are now two people left behind. Of course in real life, these two people would be adults and one of them would drive behind the bus. However, the question is examining the child's understanding of what to actually do when presented with a decimal as part of an answer.

Auditing your own subject knowledge (page 98)

1.

Fraction	Percentage	Decimal
½	50%	0.5
1/8	12.5%	0.125
3/4	75%	0.75
3/8	37.5%	0.375
1/10	10%	0.1
1½	150%	1.5
1/4	25%	0.25

2. 0.07 1/10 1/8 0.3 2/5 1/2 3/4

3. 24 children

4. 5

5. 0.003

6. 6

Children's use of language related to shape (page 100)

Area of shape, space or measure	Associated vocabulary	
	5 years old	**11 years old** (new words from the left column)
Measures of size/ length/distance	size length, width, height, depth long, short, tall and comparisons – longer, shorter, taller and superlatives – longest, shortest, highest deep, shallow	circumference kilometre (km), metre (m) mile, yard ruler, compasses
Time	days of the week morning, afternoon, evening, night today, yesterday tomorrow hour, o'clock	half past, quarter past/to 24-hour clock, 12-hour clock digital/analogue clock always, never, sometimes, often, usually Greenwich Mean Time, British Summer Time
2D shape	circle, triangle, square, rectangle, star	equilateral triangle, isosceles triangle, scalene triangle rhombus, kite, parallelogram, trapezium pentagon, hexagon, octagon, polygon, quadrilateral

Adapted from DfEE (2000)

Note: This list is not exhaustive, just some examples of key words or phrases.

Progress checklist

Have you:

○ completed the reflective tasks in this chapter and looked at the answers and explanations?

○ followed up some of the readings?

○ audited your maths subject knowledge and set yourself some targets?

○ tried a practice numeracy QTS test or the real one?

JARGON BUSTER

Early learning goals (ELGs):　these are expectations for what most children will be able to do by the end of the Foundation Stage.

Foundation Stage:　this is the phase of education prior to Key Stage 1. The Early Years Foundation Stage framework sets out requirements for all early years providers working with children under five and can be found at: www.webarchive.nationalarchives. gov.uk/20130401151715/https:// www.education.gov.uk/publications/ eOrderingDownload/EYFS%20 Statutory%20Framework.pdf.

Key Stages:　the primary curriculum is taught in two age phases: Key Stage 1 addresses Years 1 and 2 (children aged 5–7) and Key Stage 2 addresses Years 3–6 (children aged 7–11).

Learning objective:　a statement that sets out exactly what the teacher intends a child to learn during a lesson or activity.

SATs (Standardised Assessment Tasks): national tests taken by all Year 6 children in England in their final year of primary school. These include formal timed tests in mathematics.

 TAKING IT FURTHER

Cotton, T (2010) *Teaching and Understanding Primary Maths*, Harlow: Pearson.

Haylock, D (2010) *Mathematics Explained for Primary Teachers*, London: Sage.

Haylock, D and Cockburn, A (2013) *Understanding Mathematics for Young Children: A Guide for Teachers of Children 3–8*, 4th edition. London: Sage.

REFERENCES

Borthwick, C (2011) Children's Perceptions of and Attitudes Towards their Mathematics Lessons. *Proceedings of the British Society for Research into Learning Mathematics*, 31(1): 37–42.

Cohen, S (2004) *Teachers' Professional Development and the Elementary Mathematics Classroom: Bringing Understanding to Light*. Mahwah, NJ: Lawrence Erlbaum Associates.

Cockcroft (1982) *Mathematics Counts: Report of the Committee of Inquiry into the Teaching of Mathematics in Schools under the Chairmanship of Dr WH Cockcroft*. London: Her Majesty's Stationery Office.

Department for Education (DfE) (2012a) *Teachers' Standards*. London: Crown Publications. Available at www.gov.uk/government/publications/teachers-standards.

Department for Education (DfE) (2012b) *Early Years Foundation Stage Profile Handbook*. London: Crown Publications.

Department for Education and Employment (DfEE) (2000) *Mathematical Vocabulary*. London: Crown Publications.

Department for Education and Skills (DfES) (2006) *Primary Framework for Literacy and Mathematics*. Nottingham: DfES Publications.

Dweck, C (2006) Is Maths a Gift? in Ceci, SJ and Williams, W (eds) *Why Aren't More Women in Science? Top Researchers Debate the Evidence*. Washington, DC: American Psychological Association.

Every Child a Chance Trust and KPMG (2008) *The Long Term Cost of Numeracy Difficulties*. Available at www.nationalnumeracy.org.uk/resources/14/index.html.

Ofsted (2012) *Made to Measure*. London: Ofsted Publications. Available at www.ofsted.gov.uk/resources/mathematics-made-measure.

Rhydderch-Evans, Z (2002) Attitude is Everything. *Mathematics Teaching*, 181: 20.

Shulman, LS (1986) Those Who Understand: Knowledge Growth in Teaching. *Educational Researcher*, 15(2): 4–31.

Williams, P (2008) *Independent Review of Primary Mathematics Teaching in Early Years Settings and Primary Schools*. Nottingham: DCSF Publications.

7

Organising the curriculum for learning

Sarah Williams

INTRODUCTION

As explored in Chapter 4, most primary schools in England must follow the national curriculum (DfE, 2013), although some – free schools and academies – can devise their own curricula. In its previous form (DfEE, 1999) the national curriculum essentially accounted for all available teaching time. However, at the time of writing, reforms are intended to reduce the level of prescription contained in the national curriculum while still retaining some form of national framework. It is the intention to maintain a common entitlement, and encourage a broad and varied curriculum, while allowing schools greater freedom and flexibility to creatively plan for its implementation. The challenge for each school is to customise this basic entitlement to learning and, in the context of government policies and initiatives, create its own distinctive and unique curriculum. This chapter provides an insight into the way the curriculum is planned and how approaches are used to inspire and engage learners.

DESIGNING THE CURRICULUM

Schools have the freedom to decide how to arrange learning in the school day. The Department for Education provides guidance suggesting how much time should be allocated to each subject but this is not statutory. It is for schools to decide how the timetable is organised, which aspects are emphasised and how subjects are taught. Subjects can be grouped, taught through themes and topics and, if strong enough links are created between subjects, children can use knowledge and skills to develop learning across the whole curriculum. The *Independent Review of the Primary Curriculum* (Rose, 2009) acknowledged that there is a place on the timetable for both specific subject lessons and thematic work.

Although there are an increasing number of specialists teaching in primary schools, on the whole most primary teachers are generalists, and plan to teach the curriculum as a whole. Many primary schools are developing innovative and flexible ways of managing the curriculum that encourage teachers to creatively respond to the needs of learners. In most cases a school will consider its values and will establish curriculum priorities and emphases through asking, *What kinds of learning are important for our children?*

The types of questions schools may consider when designing their curriculum include:

- What might need to be added to the statutory curriculum for a school to meet its aims?

o Which subjects will be taught separately and which will be combined with other subjects?

o What cross-curricular opportunities are there to apply and develop children's skills, knowledge and understanding?

o When will subjects and topic-based units of work be taught?

o How can the design of the curriculum ensure continuity and assist children to make a smooth transfer from one age phase to the next?

Schools may provide additional opportunities that enhance learning in national curriculum subjects, such as visits to theatres, museums and galleries, residential trips and inter-school sports competitions. Clubs and activities based on interests such as cookery, ICT and sports are often held before or after school. Each school makes its own decisions about additional provision within or outside teaching time. Bearing in mind that these activities are voluntary, they may carry a charge for families and may have implications related to transport for children with special needs.

School-based example

Every Child a Swimmer programme

Phillimore is an average sized primary school in Darnall in the east end of Sheffield serving a diverse community. The breakdown of the school population in terms of ethnicity is as follows:

Black – Somali	11%
Bangladeshi	13%
White British	23%
Pakistani	30%
White Eastern European	14%
Other	9%

As the community has changed over the years, swimming has become a priority. Less than 4 per cent of pupils at the school currently attend regular private swimming lessons. School swimming lessons provided by the city council have therefore become more important. However, with the knowledge that the core offer of ten lessons was not enough to get non-swimmers swimming (historically 10 per cent of pupils were able to swim 25 metres – the minimum distance required by the national curriculum), concern started to grow about a generation of non-swimmers growing up in Darnall.

A variety of programmes were put into action, ranging from a short but intensive programme in July 2008 where each Year 6 pupil attended school swimming lessons every day for two weeks at the nearest pool (four miles away), to a mobile swimming pool provided by 'Pools to Schools' arriving at the school in October 2008. The mobile pool removed the need for transport and allowed every child in the school at least one lesson per week and a minimum of 15 lessons for those in Year 5 and 6. While it cannot be claimed that the mobile pool increased the number of swimmers, it brought great excitement and interest to a community that was in danger of being overlooked in terms of swimming. Parents, grandparents, councillors, an MP and the director of Children's Services visited during the six-week period the pool was in the school. The physical education (PE) co-ordinator recognised the importance of maintaining attention on swimming as a curriculum subject and recommended the creation of a sustainable programme that allowed each year group sufficient time in the water to reach age-related expectations. Schools in other parts of Sheffield would not have to devote as much time to this part of the curriculum as a high proportion of children already attend private swimming lessons.

Reports were written and presented to the head teacher and governors, recommending a way forward. Currently (April 2013), Phillimore has 180 pupils attending school swimming lessons.

Based on study of the last four years of swimming programmes, the school decided to implement a whole year of continuous school swimming lessons in Year 4 with top-up lessons in Year 5 if needed. This is delivered as part of the PE curriculum to meet the statutory requirements of the national curriculum. Feedback from pupils and parents has highlighted a change in attitude towards swimming that is now accepted as a vital life skill and features as one of the most popular subjects on the school's timetable. However, the most important step forward is that it is now recognised by school staff and governors that additional swimming lessons can make a difference to the ability of pupils at Phillimore to learn to swim.

Jo Searle

This example provides an insight into the process of decision-making that helped shape part of the curriculum in a Sheffield primary school. It takes into account locally identified needs as well as statutory requirements to teach swimming and support Key Stage 2 children to swim 25 metres unaided. This decision was based on knowledge that children were not swimming for a number of reasons specific to this community, and through local consultation a decision was taken to place greater emphasis on this aspect of the curriculum. Not all schools would adopt this approach. Indeed, some schools may offer limited access to swimming due to a high number of successful swimmers and devote this time to other areas of the curriculum that are of greater priority.

Reflective task

When you are in school, find out how the school has adapted the curriculum to meet the needs of the community it serves. Consider areas of the curriculum that may be influenced by the needs of a specific community and how the curriculum may differ in faith-based schools.

The following article considers how the school curriculum responds to the needs of the community and reflects the needs of its students. As you read this article consider how the curriculum is enacted in the school.

Cowie, B, Hipkins, R, Keown, P and Boyd, S (2011) *The Shape of Curriculum Change: A Short Discussion of Key Findings from the Curriculum Implementation Studies (CIES) Project.* New Zealand Council for Educational Research. Available at www.nzcer.org.nz/research/publications/shape-curriculum-change.

HOW MUCH TIME NEEDS TO BE SPENT FOCUSING ON EACH SUBJECT?

Many schools devote considerable energy to deciding how much time should be allocated across the curriculum to provide a broad and balanced curriculum while ensuring subjects are allocated sufficient time to develop key skills. Sometimes two subjects are taught together while some subjects may only be taught in alternate terms. One important timetabling consideration is the availability of appropriate staff including teaching assistants, hall space and specialist equipment such as musical instruments. The curriculum may be organised to ensure that these various resources are not being called on at the same time by various classes. This may seem like a minor consideration but when planning an innovative curriculum providing choice or utilising specialist support, it is essential that timetabling is carefully managed.

Teacher voice

Planning for music across the school

As subject leader for music, I regularly review and monitor the provision for music and shape it to suit the children it is delivered to. I identify the needs of learners and design a suitable curriculum that reflects the requirements of the national curriculum and current trends in music education.

The school curriculum is shaped in response to the whole-school development plan. This is regularly revisited to ensure that all developments are used as a vehicle to move the school forward. Key Skills are included in the medium-term plans for all subjects, including music; subject leaders monitor these on an annual basis for coverage and application.

My teaching is focused in Key Stage 2, although I support class teachers in Key Stage 1 in the development of their ability to deliver the curriculum. I design the curriculum for the whole school based on the national curriculum and monitor the plans of teachers for good teaching and learning in music.

Resourcing, particularly in terms of space, is an issue in my present role. I teach music lessons in the classroom of each class and, subsequently, I am required to move instruments around the school to deliver lessons. Classroom space is often committed to table groups rather than floor-based, whole-class and small group learning.

Music is an expensive subject to resource, and part of the role of the music specialist is to justify and secure funding to maintain the instruments available in school. When good quality instruments are available, good quality teaching and learning can take place. Teachers are inspired to experiment with, and use, a wider range of resources.

The importance of progress in literacy and maths will continue to pose challenge to other curriculum areas, and music is no exception. While respecting the imperative to drive high quality teaching and learning in the core subjects, it is also the role of the music specialist to repeatedly remind school leadership of the importance of music as having known benefits to the developing brain and in providing a balanced curriculum. Music is particularly important to children in areas of socio-economic deprivation, to those with Special Educational Needs and EAL [English as an Additional Language] learners.

In a typical week, all children in my school receive approximately one hour of music led either by myself or by their class teacher. In addition, other curriculum areas are complemented by the use of music, eg, singing in maths. Children also meet once a week for hymn practice that lasts for 45 minutes.

Additional provisions for music-making activities in school include: whole-class, small group and individual instrumental lessons; involvement in local community and city-wide singing ventures, eg, Spring for Singing 2013; extra-curricular drummers club; and music ICT [information and communication technology] club. Often, for children to take part in these activities, instruments are borrowed or hired. Musical instrument acquisition and parental wealth are possibly the greatest barriers to extra music tuition, although for children who are noted to have a particular strength in this area, a budget can usually be justified to develop their individual gift and skill.

Bernadette Twomey, primary music specialist

Reflective task

When you are next in a school, talk to teachers about how the curriculum is organised.

○ What has informed the school's priorities?

○ How are resources allocated to different subject areas?

CROSS-CURRICULAR LEARNING

Once a school has a clear understanding of its values and how the curriculum will be organised, it can start to make decisions about how to successfully integrate subjects across the curriculum. Cross-curricular learning involves drawing together key concepts, attitudes, skills and knowledge of different subjects and applying them to a single idea or problem. Links may be forged between and across subjects where there are common areas of learning, such as a design technology project that links art, science and geography focusing on the design of a sustainable product. Cross-curricular links can provide a focus for work within and between subjects and help make learning exciting and relevant to children. Often we see cross-curricular teaching and learning described as integrated or topic-based work.

A key feature of cross-curricular learning involves children learning together in an interactive way. Children should not only be encouraged to develop as independent learners but also learn through interaction with others. Children learn as much, if not more, through social interaction that is effectively supported by adults (Kerry, 2011, p 46). This supports the belief that children are not just active learners but are active agents in their own learning. Cross-curricular approaches can create opportunities for children to pursue their own interests and generate original ideas. They encourage a skill-based curriculum, focused on developing interpersonal and intrapersonal skills and thinking skills.

Cross-curricular methods are sometimes criticised for diminishing the quality of teaching of specific subjects (Barnes, 2011, p 206). Cross-curricular approaches are, however, like many practices, ineffective when teaching is confusing and creates misconceptions. This happens due to poor practice and preparation, not because of the integration of subjects. High quality cross-curricular teaching arguably requires an increased depth of subject knowledge in order to understand the ways in which children learn particular subjects so links can be made between subjects. This does not mean that teachers need to know everything about every subject but they should be familiar with the distinctive features of each subject and the associated key skills.

The best cross-curricular learning opportunities promote creative thinking and enquiry and may be stimulated by:

○ play;

○ a visit;

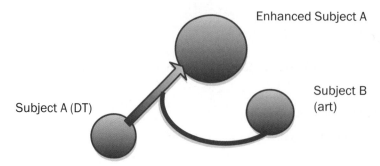

Figure 7.1 Hierarchical method for cross-curricular development (reproduced by kind permission of Jonathan Barnes)

○   a whole class discussion;

○   an incident.

The most common way in which we develop cross-curricular learning is through a hierarchical method of progressing one subject by using prior learning and aspects of another subject. Barnes (2011) uses the model shown in Figure 7.1 to illustrate a hierarchical method for cross-curricular development.

This model is illustrated through the following example, which demonstrates the benefits of cross-curricular learning. As you read this example identify subject A and subject B and consider how subject B is used to enhance subject A.

School-based example

Math-letics

This project was developed by a school sport partnership with the aim of enriching the curriculum through the use of physical activity.

Math-letics is a physical programme of activities aimed at engaging Year 2 and 3 children in numeracy activities. The programme includes a number of opportunities focused on developing children's confidence in using a range of mathematical processes, in order to deepen and broaden their knowledge, skills and understanding when addressing a number of problems. Activities include:

○ relay races;

○ running for distance and time;

○ shot-put chest push;

○ soft javelin throw;

○ long jump;

○ speed jump;

○ vertical jump.

Children were challenged to apply suitable mathematics accurately, communicate results and ideas effectively, and select appropriate mathematical tools and methods, including through the use of ICT. The process of combining understanding and experiences helped children to construct new knowledge and enhance enjoyment and motivation.

Following this programme of activities, learners were challenged to run an athletics event for younger children. They had to call on skills developed through their own experience to accurately measure and officiate during the younger children's games. This provided opportunities for children to develop new skills that may not have already been developed in the previous activities, such as problem-solving, communication and leadership skills.

One teacher involved in the programme described the activity as *inclusive and stimulating* and believed that the approach provided a range of learners with challenging opportunities to explore key mathematical concepts, and a highly motivating opportunity to engage learners, drawing on the children's enthusiasm for physical activities.

Craig Malkin

Reflective task

Consider the above example of cross-curricular learning.

○ Did both subjects benefit from this approach or could single subject teaching have been more beneficial?

○ What role do you think motivation played in the apparent success of this example?

A CREATIVE CURRICULUM

For children to understand new information they must become actively involved. Through a process of exploration, children often develop skills in problem-solving while fostering creativity. Creativity has been shown to improve motivation, self-esteem and children's construction of knowledge (Jesson, 2012, p 11). Creative approaches to teaching can empower and encourage children to use their imagination. Without creative approaches to stimulating learning in the classroom we run the risk of boring children and limiting their potential. Finding ways to develop children's creative skills is vital in motivating children and developing their thirst for knowledge and new skills. This can be facilitated through a number of experiences that encourage learners to question and explore.

A creative curriculum looks to excite imagination so that children advance beyond their present understanding and contemplate worlds possible as well as actual. It seeks to engage learners and promote collaborative creative partnerships, and empower them through experiential learning. Creative approaches can enable children to translate experiences into meaning and develop independent thoughts. Creative approaches rely on a teacher's ability to personalise learning while making imaginative connections with the class as a whole.

Classroom example

The Snail and the Whale

The Snail and the Whale (Donaldson, 2001) is a story about the adventures shared between a snail and a whale until disaster strikes and the whale becomes stranded. A classroom teacher shared this story with a group of children. After some discussion the teacher produced a photo of an adventure she went on to help to save some stranded whales. The teacher went on to encourage the children to bring in a book that meant something to them and recall who gave them the book, or who had read the book to them.

Creative teachers allow opportunities for children to revisit prior learning and experiences to help connect with new learning in a personal way. Examples such as *The Snail and the Whale* may appear to stray from the requirements of the curriculum and may appear to prioritise children's social and personal learning over subject outcomes. However, making these connections serves to motivate learners and encourage greater creativity and focus.

Reflective task

o   What do you think creativity is?

o   Can you recall a time when you used your creative skills to approach something in a new or different way?

o   Do you think it is possible to teach creativity?

Consider these questions while you view the following YouTube clip exploring the role of creativity: www.youtube.com/watch?v=iG9CE55wbtY.

Teachers can develop creative classrooms through:

o   rewarding curiosity and exploration;

o   building motivation;

o   encouraging risk-taking;

o   having high expectations of children's ability;

o   providing children with opportunities to discover and have choice.

DEVELOPING CHILDREN'S THINKING

Benjamin Bloom was an educational psychologist who made significant contributions to educational theory. He developed a hierarchy that classified different learning objectives and skills to support educators to develop and challenge students. Bloom's *Taxonomy* (Bloom and Krathwohl, 1956) classifies thinking according to cognitive levels of complexity and is often described as a stairway, leading students towards higher-level thinking. It is hierarchical, meaning that learning at the higher levels is dependent on having attained knowledge and skills at lower levels. Bloom's *Taxonomy* consists of six increasingly complex levels that assist in setting objectives and evaluating learners' cognitive abilities. These levels include:

o   knowledge: retrieving and recalling information;

o   comprehension: restating in own words, summarising;

o   application: using information to solve problems;

o   analysis: determining how things relate to one another;

o   synthesis: making judgements and demonstrating critical thinking;

o   evaluation: making decisions and understanding values.

Bloom's Taxonomy works on the assumption that for a child to be able to successfully evaluate, they would need to have the necessary information, understand the information they had, be able to apply it, be able to analyse it, synthesise it and then eventually evaluate it. The following example illustrates this by providing examples linked to these stages.

Example: Goldilocks and the three bears

o   Remember *(knowledge)*: describe where Goldilocks lived.

o   Understand *(comprehension)*: summarise what the Goldilocks story was about.

o   Apply *(application)*: construct a theory as to why Goldilocks went into the house.

o   Analyse *(analysis)*: differentiate between how Goldilocks reacted and how you would react in each story event.

o   Evaluate *(synthesis)*: assess whether or not you think this really happened to Goldilocks.

o   Create *(evaluation)*: compose a song, skit or poem to convey the Goldilocks story in a new form.

Reflective task

When observing in a classroom, Bloom's *Taxonomy* can be an effective tool to assist you to evaluate learning. Use the following prompts to help you to identify the stages children are working through and the level of challenge within activities.

o Are tasks encouraging children to remember and recall relevant knowledge from long-term memory?

o Are tasks encouraging children to develop understanding through interpreting and explaining information?

o Are children applying or testing a theory?

o Are children analysing information, determining how the parts relate to one another?

o Are children evaluating, checking, critiquing and making their own judgements?

o Are children planning, producing or creating new forms of learning?

LEARNING THROUGH TALK

Children learn not only through doing, but also by talking about what they are doing. Talk assists children to develop ideas and comment on what they observe. We have discussed the importance of creativity and working in a social context with the assumption that children have the necessary communication skills to fully engage in creative and collaborative learning opportunities. In primary schools many children are only just beginning to learn through their reading and writing. Talk is therefore the medium in which most learning occurs. Jerome Bruner (1986, p 72) explored the notion that children develop their own knowledge through experience with the environment. He believed that, as far as teaching is concerned, good teachers should try to encourage children to discover their own meaning by themselves. Bruner believed that the teacher should engage children in active dialogue by asking focused questions and providing appropriate materials. The role of the teacher is therefore to facilitate learning, and talk is critical in this process.

The work of Lev Vygotsky (1978) is considered to be a key influence on teachers' understanding of the learning process. Vygotsky's theory promotes learning where children play an active role in the learning process, and the role of the teacher is to collaborate with the learners to help construct meaning. This is often also described as a 'reciprocal approach'. According to Vygotsky, children develop skills such as speech and writing to engage in social environments and help them to communicate needs. Vygotsky believed that once they had these skills they could then develop higher order thinking skills. If we take his approach we can also assume that talk between children is likewise advantageous if modelled and encouraged by the teacher.

Dialogic teaching and exploratory talk

Two kinds of talk you may observe when in the classroom are dialogic teaching and exploratory talk. During dialogic teaching you may observe a child sharing an opinion or fact, and the teacher questioning the child to contribute more and develop thinking. Questions might include *What if...? Would anyone else like to challenge that?* Teachers also work to promote exploratory talk between children without adult support (Mercer and Hodgkinson, 2008). For this talk to be meaningful, children must share a common purpose and motivation. This is often successfully observed when a group of children are faced with a problem or challenge. With young children, teachers may provide a structure for this talk. They may, for example, model questions or work with children to create group rules for managing discussion such as taking turns and not talking over others.

Enquiry-based learning

You may encounter planning and teaching approaches that are based around questions. These 'enquiries' are characterised by the use of a key question that stimulates research, and further questions that are driven by the children's interests. Enquiries may apply to all the learning and teaching that takes place over a period of time, or may apply to one specific subject area or theme. Generic skills relating to teamwork and researching and presenting information are developed through the enquiry process. A vital part of the enquiry will be reflection that engages children in evaluation of their learning throughout (Jesson, 2012, p 131).

Philosophy for children

Philosophy for Children (P4C) is another approach that stimulates talk and is based on enquiry. Children take part in focused philosophical enquiries in which open questions are explored through structured sessions in communities of enquiry. The sessions are usually organised using a 'circle time' approach and take place regularly, perhaps weekly. In P4C the quality of questions chosen for discussion is vital and consideration of this is part of the P4C process. To an inexperienced observer, P4C may seem to be a relatively easy approach: children sit in a circle and discuss questions, and the teacher is able to take a facilitating rather than an instructing role. However, P4C is highly demanding and requires considerable understanding and skill from the facilitator to ensure a session is worthwhile and not a superficial exercise. As with any approach that has a specific focus and time, it is only through its application across children's learning that impact and benefit will be felt. So with P4C, the benefits to children's thinking – through the development of their curiosity, criticality and reflection, and their ability to express and share ideas and listen and understand others – will be spread through other areas of learning if the teacher helps children to notice and make connections.

MOTIVATION

A key influence on what we do and how we engage with learning is motivation. Motivation is the process that guides our behaviours in many domains including school. Behaviourists explain motivation in terms of both positive and negative reinforcement and these factors are highly influential. Most people are motivated to be fit and healthy. However, past experiences may provoke a negative response when you put on your trainers and head out to the gym.

Behaviourism is based around the notion that reaction is specific to a particular relationship or situation. John Watson was the first psychologist to use the term behaviourism and his work is built on the early work of a physiologist Ivan Pavlov, who documented the responses of a dog to external stimuli. Pavlov's initial experiments conditioned dogs to salivate at the sound of a bell. His initial experiments found that a dog salivated when they ate or had sight of food. He began sounding a bell whenever food was presented to the dog and eventually the dog was salivating at the sound of the bell regardless of the presence of food. The dog's behaviour had been modified in the same way that our behaviour is sometimes modified by the smell of a roast dinner or the sound of a dentist's drill.

The work of Watson and Pavlov has influenced how we motivate children and set out expectations of behaviour, and, crucially, highlights how teacher motivation can model a response to certain activities and subjects. The ways in which a teacher designs and presents the curriculum have a substantial impact on the response and motivation of learners (Barnes, 2011, p 164).

Figure 7.2 TASC wheel (reproduced by kind permission of Belle Wallace)

Enquiry-based approaches

TASC, designed by Belle Wallace (2001, 2002a, 2002b, 2003; Wallace and Maker, 2004; Wallace et al, 2008), is an enquiry-based approach used in many schools that draws on many of the ideas discussed so far within this chapter. TASC stands for Thinking Actively in a Social Context and its aim is to develop children's problem-solving skills with the support of a clearly defined set of steps. The emphasis is on solving real-life problems, drawing on many of the cognitive, creative and communication skills previously discussed. TASC is a generic framework used in many schools to help with the development of thinking and problem-solving within the curriculum. It is an approach that can be applied to all areas of the curriculum and helps to consolidate existing and good practice.

When considering the development of a creative curriculum that facilitates cross-curricular learning, models such as TASC are an effective way of guiding learners while developing social and communication skills. Children often find problem-solving exciting and enjoy the responsibility that often comes with a problem-solving approach. An evaluation of TASC carried out by Davies (2008) showed that TASC:

o   helped children to stay focused and demonstrate high levels of interaction with peers;

o   encouraged children to support each other;

o   provided opportunities for children to question ideas.

TASC is illustrated with the support of a wheel (see Figure 7.2), which guides children through various problems with creativity and independence.

Classroom example

TASC in action

Children are not eating their school dinners. They have been asked to design a healthy sandwich that most children would enjoy and which could be easily added to the dinner menu. They use the TASC wheel to plan an enquiry.

○ **Step one:** Gather/organise – what do you already know about this problem?

○ **Step two:** What is the task? What do you need to achieve?

○ **Step three:** Generate – how many different sandwich ideas can you come up with?

○ **Step four:** Decide on your best idea.

○ **Step five:** Implement – give it a go and try out your sandwich with other people in the school.

○ **Step six:** Evaluate how well you did and if your sandwich will be successful.

○ **Step seven:** Communicate your ideas with others and see what can be done with your ideas.

○ **Step eight:** What have you learnt from this experience? Can you use these skills again?

LEARNING STIMULI

Teachers tend to engage children through a number of different approaches to meet the needs of various learners, to keep learning experiences fresh and avoid repetition. An alternative approach to TASC that provides less structure and is often preferred by Key Stage 1 teachers is an approach referred to as learning hooks, or learning stimuli. We have already touched on this approach through the example of Goldilocks, using Bloom's *Taxonomy*.

Magical unexpected moments in the classroom can encourage children to develop their sense of wonder about the world. Science is a great context for this as it allows the children to test ideas as scientists themselves and, sometimes, be surprised by what happens. This concept can however be applied to many areas of the curriculum. Knowing what ignites your children's imaginations and motivation to learn should be at the centre of every learning experience. Building on children's interests is the key to high levels of engagement and to finding ways to hook them into learning. Animations, films, visuals, drama and art are great ways to add creativity and excitement to lessons and make children feel valued as learners.

Classroom example

Learning hooks

A teacher arranged for a rabbit to suddenly appear in a classroom one morning. The children were surprised and intrigued to find out where the rabbit had come from and what they needed to do. The teacher guided the children's thinking through effective use of questioning.

○ Where do we think the rabbit might have come from?

○ What do we need to do to care for the rabbit?

○ Who can help us to find the rabbit's home?

○ Who has knowledge of rabbits that can help us?

○ How can we keep the rabbit safe until we find its home?

The questions posed by the teacher helped shape the focus for learning and identify cross-curricular links. Through careful planning the teacher guided the children's process of enquiry to develop key concepts, attitudes and skills linked to the learning stimulus. The class was encouraged to explore learning linked to key areas of the curriculum such as design and technology as they discussed how they would keep the rabbit safe. The class was guided through a TASC model of enquiry as they researched the needs of a rabbit. Various sources were used to support this process including internet searches and a prearranged interview in the classroom with a local vet. With this new knowledge, the class then proceeded to build an appropriate shelter for the rabbit, catering for all of its needs. Construction materials were tested and the children experimented with various techniques to assemble and join components to make a hutch.

Reflective task

This example briefly considers how a learning stimulus can challenge and motivate learners, draw on children's interests and build on prior knowledge. Can you think of any other areas of the curriculum that could have been included in this activity day?

CONCLUSION

This chapter has identified a number of common factors that assist with planning and implementing a creative curriculum. This is by no means a definitive list. Many schools are regularly engaging with a review process that monitors the impact of teaching on children's learning. Schools need to ensure that statutory requirements are being met, that the needs of learners are being considered and that all children are making progress. A creative curriculum is one that excites learners, empowers them through discovery and leads them to find new meaning in a changing world. Teachers have a highly complex role in facilitating such a curriculum. This relies on considerable skills in planning and teaching to enrich the programmes of study within the national curriculum. Teachers need to develop pedagogical skills that facilitate a creative learning environment that challenges learners.

This chapter has explored the many influences that inform what we teach and how we teach. It has drawn on the work of key theorists who have influenced teachers' pedagogy and values. You have been encouraged to critically consider your values and the skills that are needed to shape a curriculum that engages and challenges all learners. When you are next in school, try to reflect on key aspects considered within this chapter such as creativity and consider the breadth and balance of the curriculum, connections between and across various subjects, and the promotion of motivation, creativity and, ultimately, children's self-esteem.

 Progress checklist

Consider what might shape a school's decisions when designing their curriculum.

○ Most primary school teachers are generalist but what could specialist teachers contribute to a school community?

○ Have you observed any cross-curricular approaches in schools? Consider some of the challenges and benefits of designing a cross-curricular approach.

○ Try to seek an opportunity to observe enquiry-based learning in school. Review some of the suggested readings and consider various ways you could guide learning using a model such as TASC.

JARGON BUSTER

Key Stages: *the primary curriculum is taught in two age phases: Key Stage 1 addresses Years 1 and 2 (children aged 5–7) and Key Stage 2 addresses Years 3–6 (children aged 7–11).*

Learning objective*:*   *a statement that sets out exactly what the teacher intends a child to learn during a lesson or activity.*

Medium-term plans*:*   *teachers produce medium-term plans that set out the learning objectives they will address during a term or half-term and the activities they anticipate using.*

Programme of study*:*   *the national curriculum includes programmes of study that set out what is to be learned in each age phase.*

 TAKING IT FURTHER

Barnes, J (2011) *Cross-Curricular Learning 3–14*. London: Sage.

Explores practical and theoretical issues linked to cross-curricular teaching and learning.

Csikszentmihalyi, M (1990) The Domain of Creativity, in Runco, M and Albert, R (eds) *Theories of Creativity*. London: Sage.

Highly influential work exploring the nature of creativity.

Jesson, J (2012) *Developing Creativity in the Primary School*. Maidenhead: Open University Press.

Introduces and explores a range of creative approaches to teaching.

REFERENCES

Barnes, J (2011) *Cross-Curricular Learning 3–14*. London: Sage.

Bloom, B S and Krathwohl, D R (1956). *Taxonomy of Educational Objectives*. New York: Longman.

Bruner, J (1986) *Actual Minds, Possible Worlds*. London: Harvard Press.

Cowie, B, Hipkins, R, Keown, P and Boyd, S (2011) *The Shape of Curriculum Change*. New Zealand: Ministry of Education.

Davies, H (2008) *An Overview of an Investigation into the Effects of Using TASC Strategies in the Development of Children's Thinking and Problem Solving Skills in Science*. Oxford: AB Academic Publishers.

Department for Education (DfE) (2013) *The National Curriculum in England: Framework Document for Consultation*. London: Crown Publications. Available at www.media. education.gov.uk/assets/files/pdf/n/national%20curriculum%20consultation%20 -%20framework%20document.pdf.

Department for Education and Employment (DfEE) (1999) *The National Curriculum*. London: HMSO. Available at www.educationengland.org.uk/documents/pdfs/1999-nc-primary-handbook.pdf.

Donaldson, J (2001) *The Snail and the Whale*. London: Macmillan Books.

Jesson, J (2012) *Developing Creativity in the Primary School*. Berkshire: Open University Press.

Kerry, J (2011) *Cross-Curricular Teaching in the Primary School*. London: Routledge.

Mercer, N and Hodgkinson, S (2008) *Exploring Talk in School*. London: Sage.

Rose, J (2009) *Independent Review of the Primary Curriculum: Final Report*. Nottingham: DCSF Publications. Available at www.webarchive.nationalarchives. gov.uk/20130401151715/https://www.education.gov.uk/publications/eOrderingDownload/Primary_curriculum_Report.pdf.

Vygotsky, L (1978) *Mind in Society*, trans. M Cole. Cambridge, MA: Harvard University Press.

Wallace, B (2001) *Teaching Thinking Skills Across the Primary Curriculum*. London: Routledge.

Wallace, B (2002a) *Teaching Thinking Skills Across the Early Years*. London: Routledge.

Wallace, B (2002b) *Teaching Thinking Skills Across the Middle Years*. London: Routledge.

Wallace, B (2003) *Using History to Develop Thinking Skills at Key Stage 2*. London: Routledge.

Wallace, B and Maker, J (2004) *Thinking Skills and Problem-Solving: An Inclusive Approach*. London: Routledge.

Wallace, B, Cave, D and Berry, A (2008) *Teaching Problem-Solving and Thinking Skills through Science*. London: Routledge.

8

Learning to learn

Jane Bartholomew

INTRODUCTION

A good teacher is a good learner!

Children from Wales Primary School in Rotherham

As you consider your learning journey towards becoming a qualified teacher, you may naturally be focusing on what you bring to teaching in terms of relevant skills, qualities and knowledge. For example, you may have skills in communication or have expertise in mathematics. Yet, as the opening comment from primary school pupils indicates, teaching is all about learning, and teachers who feel passionate about learning will tend to be the inspirational individuals who we may remember from our own school days. Learning is a process in which we are constantly engaged, whether we are in formal educational settings or as we go about our daily lives and even when we are asleep (Claxton, 2005).

This chapter will familiarise you with ways in which learning is placed at the centre of teaching, beginning with an introduction to different perspectives of learning in primary education. It will then go on to explore how primary schools develop effective learners. In addition to this practical focus, you will be asked to reflect upon how you feel about yourself as a learner, as this will have implications for you as someone who is interested in teaching. By the end of the chapter you will have an overview of learning in primary education. When you spend time in schools, you will be able to recognise teaching approaches that focus on learning, place them within a meaningful context and understand the thinking behind the classroom practice you observe. This will enable you to identify areas that you may need to explore further in order to prepare for your application for initial teacher preparation.

WAYS OF LOOKING AT LEARNING IN PRIMARY SCHOOLS

Consider your experiences of learning from your earliest days: you learned to walk, use language and communicate with others. Since entering formal education you will have learned knowledge and gained skills and understanding across a range of subjects while developing social skills that underpin human interaction. So it is evident that humans possess the capacity to be effective learners.

You may have come across educational psychologists and researchers who have contributed to our understanding of how we learn. Learning is a highly complex area that relates to a wide field of disciplines. Our understanding of learning is constantly being updated as new perspectives on the subject are developed through research in areas such as neuroscience (Illeris, 2009). For the purposes of this book, we can think of learning as involving the acquisition of skills and knowledge and the development of attitudes and understanding. Primary practice tends to reflect the idea that we construct knowledge and understanding and build upon prior experiences (Pritchard, 2009). Teaching and learning approaches are also influenced by theories of learning that emphasise the importance of social interaction. In addition, understanding of children's thinking, as well as their social, emotional and physical needs, influences how children are taught from their early years to adolescence.

Reflective task

○ How would you define learning?

○ When you are next in a school, ask children what they understand by learning. How do their answers vary and what views around learning do they reflect?

○ As they progress through school, what do you notice about how children change in terms of their relationships and their thinking?

In understanding learning, you need to consider how both internal and external factors impact on the process. Internal factors can include our disposition towards learning. For example, the way in which we feel about our capacity to learn is a key factor in how effectively we learn (Adams, 2009). External factors include the ways in which teachers and practitioners facilitate a climate for learning. For example, the classroom environment can have a major impact on the extent to which children feel secure and relaxed as they go about their work and play (Duffy, 2006). Aspects of these internal and external influences on learning will be looked at in more detail later in this chapter.

As you spend time in school, you may come across approaches that are influenced by other perspectives on learning. Below we will take a critical look at three of the most popular of these: VAK (learning styles), multiple intelligences and brain-based learning.

VAK (learning styles)

You may hear teachers talk about planning for different learning styles. This refers to the idea that there are three types of learning styles: visual, auditory and kinaesthetic (VAK) and that people have a natural inclination towards one of these three styles of learning (Dixie, 2011). So a visual learner will favour learning through the use of maps, diagrams and other forms of imagery; an auditory learner will respond well to discussion, stories and musical stimulation; while a kinaesthetic learner finds activities that involve touch and movement particularly helpful (Dixie, 2011).

Criticism has been levelled at the VAK approach due to questions around its scientific credibility and the danger inherent in labelling children as preferring one particular learning style (Franklin, 2006; Sharp et al, 2008). An alternative way of looking at this is that learners need to be resourceful through being able to learn through a range of modes: for example, through speaking and listening, using and accessing images, and through physical exploration and practice. When you begin your initial teacher preparation, it is likely that you will be aware of references to learning styles. It is advisable, therefore, to maintain a healthily critical atti-tude towards this idea while being aware of the importance of multisensory teaching and learning approaches. Multisensory teaching provides all children with opportunities to learn using a range of senses through, for example, first-hand experiences such as educational visits, learning outdoors and the provision of a range of quality classroom resources.

Multiple intelligences

Howard Gardner (1993) proposed that we possess a range of intelligences as opposed to just one, overarching intelligence. So, in addition to intelligences that relate to math-ematics (logical mathematic intelligence) and literacy (linguistic intelligence), an individ-ual may also, for example, be musically intelligent or interpersonally intelligent. Primary practice that reflects Gardner's theory seeks to enable children to develop and show their understanding through a range of intelligences. Gardner's ideas have been popularised for application within primary schools and you may come across displays and teachers' planning that refer to different intelligences (Pritchard, 2009). As with the VAK approach, this perspective emphasises that it is important for teachers to be aware of children's abilities and talents across a wide range of areas in order to teach inclusively.

Neuroscience

Scientific research can inform our understanding of how learning takes place at a neuro-logical level within the brain. A finding that has implications for education is that the brain is 'plastic'. This means that it is capable of growth and response to the environ-ment throughout our lives (Blakemore and Frith, 2005). This supports the idea that we can be effective learners, capable of improving our ability to learn at any age. In recent years, approaches to teaching and learning have been developed that claim to be based upon brain research. However, the bridge required to link neuroscience to educa-tion is considerable. So-called 'brain-based' approaches towards teaching and learning may contain useful practical advice. However, claims about their basis in neuroscience should be viewed critically in order to avoid misunderstandings about the brain and potentially misguided practice that may lead from these (Howard-Jones et al, 2009).

Reflective task

○   Have you come across VAK, multiple intelligences or brain-based learning in practice?

○   How do children seem to respond to these approaches?

○   Do you notice music and song being used in classrooms?

○   How physically active are children in lessons and sessions? Do you notice any differences between early years settings and primary classrooms?

○   How do you rate your knowledge and understanding of relevant educational theory? Perhaps you have studied psychology and so feel familiar with theory around learning. Does this give you confidence in your understanding of how children learn?

WAYS OF LOOKING AT LEARNING IN PRIMARY SCHOOLS: FROM THEORY TO PRACTICE

In the early years of childhood, it could be argued that our readiness to learn is at its most evident. We are disposed towards exploration and play, enabling us to develop our understanding of the world around us. Children look for meaning in their experiences and encounters and are naturally curious (Duffy, 2006). This is often demonstrated by their propensity to ask questions.

Scenario

Does water float?

A three-year-old is having his bath at the end of the day. Over the last few weeks he has been fascinated by the way that some of his bath toys float but others sink. One evening, he suddenly looks up and asks *does water float?*

We will return to the central role curiosity plays in learning later in the chapter but for now, this example serves to illustrate how young children are already primed for learning. However, perhaps because of the systems and routines associated with education on a large scale, children's creativity and their motivation to learn can become weakened. Ivan Illich, a philosopher and commentator on education, went so far as to say that our *right to learn* is *curtailed by the obligation to attend school* (Illich, 1973, p 7). This reflects a concern that, as children progress through the educational system, they become increasingly dependent on teachers and become deskilled as learners in the process.

Schools and settings in which the needs of children are central, and which value play and creativity, will help to address these concerns. Approaches that support children in tapping into their innate creativity and disposition to learn play a key role in developing effective learners (Duffy, 2006).

Reflective task

- What kind of impact do you think school had on you as a learner?
- What do you think of the idea that school can deskill us?
- Are you aware of how children feel about school?

Of course, reasons for a child's lack of attainment and apparent disengagement with learning within the classroom are varied and complex. Earlier, the fact that learning is influenced by external and internal factors was identified and Chapter 9 will explore the barriers that exist to children's learning. It is widely recognised, however, that for all children, approaches that encourage children to 'learn about learning' are effective in raising standards (Higgins et al, 2012).

Learning about learning

In our school, everything's about learning. The children are steeped in learning here.

Diane O'Leary, head teacher of Wales Primary School, Rotherham

Diane's choice of the word *steeped* gives a real sense of the children being immersed in learning and that learning must pervade everything we do. So what does 'steeping' children in learning look like? In order to develop effective learning, schools may do some or all of the following:

○   make the *process* of learning explicit;

○   integrate practices that highlight learning into the daily routine;

○   concentrate upon skills, processes and behaviours associated with learning.

Scenario

Focusing on behaviours associated with learning

The staff at an infant school wanted to encourage the children to be more resourceful in their learning. Resourcefulness includes the ability to solve problems and be curious and so is a key aspect of learning (Claxton, 2002). The staff decided that a good way to help children understand the idea of 'resourcefulness' was to use a puppet called Rosie Resourceful. Rosie 'visited' classrooms and 'talked' about how she dealt with getting stuck at her work and how she gained help when she needed it. In this way, the children were able to understand the concept and used Rosie as a model for being resourceful so that when they were stuck with something, they could ask themselves what Rosie would do. This helped them to solve problems and manage their learning.

Such approaches are often referred to as 'learning to learn' and focus upon learning skills and dispositions that are applicable in any situation, at any stage in our lives. For example, effective learners may draw upon their resourcefulness whether playing with construction bricks at home, building a den with friends, writing a story in the classroom or collaborating with other students to produce a plan for a lesson. Thus, pupils are aware of themselves as learners and motivated to learn (Deakin Crick, 2007).

You may have come across the terms 'learning to learn' or 'assessment for learning'. These approaches are both underpinned by the notion of meta-cognition, which means thinking about thinking. Meta-cognitive approaches encourage children to think about their thinking and learning so that they develop a sense of ownership of their learning, which in turn can increase levels of motivation and self-esteem. Research indicates that approaches which make learning explicit are effective and worthwhile (Higgins et al, 2012). Learning-to-learn approaches focus upon *how* we are learning as opposed to *what* we are learning and upon the *process* of learning as much the *outcome*.

Teacher voice

Perspectives on the learning process

Cathy Rowland, head teacher of Dobcroft Infant School, Sheffield:

We focus here on the importance of the process of learning (what goes on along the way to completing a piece of work, for example), instead of just 'getting the right answer'.

Amy, student teacher:

Teachers are always referring to the learning process. I'll say things to the children like: If you go straight to your brain and the answer's not there, then you are learning – because you're having to find something out. *In mathematics, we really tried to make the thinking process explicit. For example we'd have visual prompts for children to help them through the stages of a problem-solving activity:*

1. *I can be systematic;*

2. *I can find possibilities;*

3. *I can spot patterns;*

4. *I can make generalisations.*

Children can refer to these visual reminders as a way of supporting themselves through the process of solving a mathematical problem, thereby increasing their independence as well as their problem-solving skills.

Embedding the language of learning

Teacher voice

Using the language of learning

Cathy, infant school head teacher:	*The language they're hearing, whether giving out positive or negative signals about learning, is the language pupils are picking up.*
Diane, primary school head teacher:	*When you go into our classrooms you will hear 'learning' being referred to constantly. It's really important that we talk to children about their learning rather than their 'doing'. For example* What were we learning in maths yesterday? *as opposed to* What were we doing in maths yesterday?

In order to raise children's awareness of their learning and practice, or meta-cognition, we need a shared language with which to discuss the process of learning. For example, some schools have adopted an approach that is structured around four key words that represent four dimensions of learning (Claxton, 2002). These are called the 'four Rs' of learning:

Resilience: the ability to persevere, even when we are finding things challenging;

Resourcefulness: the ability to help ourselves and solve problems;

Reciprocity: the ability to work effectively with others and learn from others;

Reflectiveness: the ability to look back at our learning and plan for next steps.

(Claxton, 2002)

The principle here is that, if shared language of learning such as 'four Rs' is used in daily interactions between children and adults, messages about learning will be reinforced and its profile will be raised. Teachers and practitioners exploit opportunities as they arise so that the language of learning becomes part of the normal discourse of the classroom. For example:

o   When a child goes to look at a classroom display to remind herself of what a rectangle looks like the teacher may comment upon the child's resourcefulness.

o   When a child is struggling to overcome a difficult or frustrating task the teacher may comment upon the child's resilience.

○   When a group of children are taking turns to share ideas the teacher may comment upon their reciprocity.

○   When a child is able to identify what helped him undertake a sustained piece of writing the teacher may comment upon the child's reflection.

The language we use with children from a very young age can have a significant impact on their understanding of their learning. Although adults may question the apparent complexity of language used, for example 'reciprocity', children seem to experience no problems in assimilating the vocabulary of learning, as long as it is used frequently, in meaningful contexts and with consistency.

Teacher voice

Reinforcing the language of learning

Cathy, infant school head teacher:

The language of effective learning is used throughout the school – in our documentation and reports, as well as in classrooms and on the playground. So parents are aware of their child's resourcefulness and resilience and the children will go home using the language. A characteristic of a significant number of children at this school was that they shied away from challenging situations, preferring to stay in their 'comfort zone'. The children were not used to the feelings associated with having to struggle with new things as their parents may have been perhaps over-eager to step in and help them. This is why we added the 5th R of 'risk-taking' to our four Rs of learning. This R encourages children to have a go and try something challenging. This can be in any context. As an example of the impact this has had here, before we brought in our extra R, we were finding that our Year 2 children were not attempting more challenging questions on the SATs papers: they were afraid to have a go at something; they were unsure of in case they got it wrong. Now that our 'risk-taking' focus is an established part of teaching and learning, children attempt all questions as they know the value of 'having a go'.

Amy, student teacher:	We have the four Bs: brain, book, buddy, boss. So the children know that if you're stuck, instead of going straight to the teacher, think about the problem to see if you can sort it out with some more effort (brain), next try a book or some information that's available (book), if that doesn't help, try asking a friend (buddy) and finally, the last resort is the teacher – the boss!

Whether we are talking about Rs, Bs or any other permutation, the principle of using language of learning consistently to develop effective learning is the same.

Reflective task

Have you come across other ways in which positive messages about learning are reinforced across schools and settings?

Learning communities: developing reciprocity

The importance of the social aspect of learning has been identified already in this chapter and this is reflected in practice that you will see on a daily basis. The reciprocal (social) nature of learning indicates that as well as being able to learn *independently*, we also need to be able to manage *inter*dependent learning effectively (Claxton, 2002). A community of learning develops out of children and adults as interdependent and intentional learners (Deakin Crick, 2007). Learning communities can operate on several levels, but to be most effective, a whole-school learning community ethos is crucial.

Reflective task

Consider the ways in which the ethos of schools and settings can support the development of effective learners.

Perhaps this will be evident in the behaviour and attitudes shown by children and adults. Some schools make their focus on learning explicit as in the case of Wales Primary School in Rotherham. At Wales, a 'learning behaviours code' has been devised by children and staff. This provides a memorable focus for improving learning behaviours:

The Wales Way: Our Learning Behaviours Code

Wanting to learn

Asking questions

Listening and thinking

Evaluating my work

Sticking at it!

A whole-school community of learning has been created in this way as all the pupils, staff and parents understand that improving learning is the focus, and the ways in which to achieve this. You will notice how this links to Cathy's comments earlier in relation to the use of a shared language.

Modelling learning

It is important to remember that good teachers are learners and that it is crucial that an enthusiasm for learning is shared with pupils. The Teachers' Standards state that teachers must *demonstrate consistently the positive attitudes, values and behaviour which are expected of pupils* and *promote a love of learning* (DfE, 2012). Many teachers will impart a 'love of learning' and are willing and able to share with children their own experiences as learners. You may notice teachers and practitioners 'learning aloud' through commenting on how they have found something challenging and how they have sought to overcome this.

Teacher voice

Modelling learning in practice

Kathryn, student teacher:

I play the guitar and would bring it in for singing with the class. Sometimes I made mistakes when I was playing, but I would draw attention to them by saying that, although playing can be tricky, I'm carrying on and persevering. The children understood that even teachers make mistakes and were patient with me, even though my mistakes interrupted our music-making!

Cathy, infant school head teacher:

All children here have the opportunity to learn to play the violin. A key part of the approach we use is that the class teacher has her own violin and is learning along with the children. So the class is aware of how the teacher has to work through difficulties with the instrument. This sends out a powerful message to children around lifelong learning and the fact that being an effective learner is something we are all developing, grown-ups as well as children!

Reflective task

o Do you consider yourself to be resilient and someone who, when faced with a challenging situation, can focus on ways of approaching this?

o How do you respond to working with others? We often expect children to work co-operatively in groups, but how challenging do we find this as adults and what do we find helpful in these situations?

o As a student teacher, you will often be asked to reflect on your experiences, as you are being encouraged to do now. Is this something in which you readily engage or do you find this process lacks focus and meaning for you? (See Chapter 4 for more on the role of reflection in teaching.)

Children as interdependent learners

The social and interactive aspects of learning are reflected in the ways that children are organised into groups and pairs in order to achieve objectives. Research over many years has highlighted the value of skilfully managed collaborative work so that children can explore their thinking together through talk (Higgins et al, 2012). In the classroom, a community of learning can be created in which everyone is actively involved in supporting each other's learning as well developing their own. This creates the exciting opportunity to really value children's contributions and thus to raise awareness of the social and reciprocal nature of learning.

Scenario

Learning to learn

Daniel needed a great deal of support in his writing and usually worked within a group that received additional adult support. His teacher was aware that he perceived himself as 'low ability' in general and compared himself unfavourably to other members of the class. Because of the focus on learning to learn, the teacher was able to highlight to Daniel, and ultimately the class, that he was very resilient and continued to try at tasks he found difficult. She also noted that he was a very resourceful learner, asking for help and making use of the writing aids available to him. In contrast, some children who found writing relatively easy would often lack resilience and give up when they found something difficult. Daniel went on to act as a 'consultant' in terms of his resilience and resourcefulness through sharing his strategies with the class, which they appreciated. As this value was placed on attitudes rather than outcome, Daniel's perception of himself became much more positive and this helped him to make significant progress in general.

Faiza in Year 2 was returning to the classroom after having undertaken a traffic survey as part of an ongoing geographical enquiry. As they neared the school hall, she said to her teacher that as a class they should spend some time reflecting upon the experience. The teacher took up Faiza's suggestion and the class sat in a circle in the hall with their clipboards to discuss what they had learnt from undertaking their survey. Faiza was very familiar with the language of 'learning to learn' and was aware of the value of reflecting upon experiences as a group in order to identify learning. Because of the community-of-learning ethos that was central to the class, she also felt confident in making suggestions that might normally be considered to be the preserve of the teacher.

These examples illustrate that we need to keep an open mind about children and their perceived abilities. They also emphasise the importance of relationships within classrooms. We will return to this later in this chapter when we consider behaviour for learning.

Developing resourceful learners

The test of intelligence is not how much we know how to do, but how we behave when we don't know what to do.

(Holt, 1984, p 203)

Scenarios

A teacher of a Year 3 class noticed a child hadn't begun writing, several minutes after the rest of the class had got underway with the activity. On being asked why he hadn't started, the child replied that he didn't have a pencil.

In a busy reception class, a child had a runny nose. She went over to the box of tissues that was placed within easy reach, took a tissue, wiped her nose and returned to her activity.

Reflective task

Consider the scenarios above. What do these illustrate in terms of the children's resourcefulness? More importantly, what could they imply about the way in which teaching and learning are organised in each setting?

Children can be resourceful if they are allowed and encouraged to be so, but it can be the case that passivity can creep in because of teaching styles that are based on control and direction. In Holt's opinion, 'when they learn in their own way and for their own reasons, children learn so much more rapidly and effectively than we could possibly teach them' (Holt, 1984, p 156).

Teacher voice

Successful learners

Diane, primary head teacher: *When I first came to this school I noticed that the children lacked independence, responsibility and a sense of ownership of their learning: they were what I would call passive learners. We asked the children about their perceptions of learning as we didn't know what the children knew about being a learner and learning. For many children when they were asked* What makes a good learner? *they responded by saying* Being good at everything. *After our work focusing on learning, the children now say that successful learners:*

- *improve by their mistakes;*
- *work well in a group/team;*
- *ask if they need help;*
- *persevere;*
- *think outside the box!*

Reflective task

- How do teachers encourage pupils' independence? For example, perhaps you will notice classroom rules and routines that encourage pupils to be resourceful.

- When you are next in a school or early years setting, ask children what they do when they become 'stuck' in their learning.

- How have you noticed children being helped to help themselves?

CURIOSITY IN THE CLASSROOM

Curiosity is a quality that is central to learning: it is the starting point for exploration and enquiry. In the introduction to this chapter we identified how this is something that drives us from our earliest years. An environment in which children's curiosity is encouraged will nurture effective learners. The Teachers' Standards recognise this, stating that teachers *must promote ... children's intellectual curiosity* (DfE, 2012, p 7). Perhaps the most powerful way in which curiosity can be nurtured is through teachers modelling their own. Here we return to the importance of your attitude towards learning and your interest in the world in which we live. If *you* are interested, it is likely that children will be too.

Curiosity is also supported through encouraging children's questions. Children's questions can be valued and encouraged in many ways including:

o   commenting on 'good questions' that children may ask
     and inviting the class to respond to them;

o   asking children in pairs to devise questions for the class to consider;

o   having a class 'Wonderwall' where children's questions are collected over a period
     of time – these may form the basis of further enquiry in the classroom or at home.

How we frame the questions we ask children is another key element in developing children's thinking and 'intellectual curiosity'. Open-ended questions or prompts are a means of encouraging children's talk for learning. Examples include:

o   I wonder why...?

o   What if...?

o   How could we find out...?

o   Can you tell me about...?

Teachers may believe that because they are explaining something, children will understand and learn. Student teachers may fall into the trap of giving long introductions to sessions when children are clearly lacking interest and attention. Children from Wales Primary School have summed this up by stating that good teachers *don't talk for ages.*

Reflective task

o   When in school, how are children's questions encouraged and valued?

o   Consider the ratio of pupil/teacher talk: is it equal? Is it weighted towards
     the teacher or the children?

o   Using some open-ended questions such as those above, how much pupil talk
     can you elicit?

There are planning and teaching approaches that are based around questions. These 'enquiries' are characterised by the use of a key question that stimulates research and further questions that are driven by the children's interests. Enquiries may apply to all the learning and teaching that takes place over a period of time, or may apply to one subject area such as geography. Generic skills relating to teamwork and finding out and presenting information are developed through the enquiry process. A vital part of the enquiry will be reflection that engages children in evaluation of their learning throughout. (See Chapter 7 for more detail on supporting children's enquiries.)

ASSESSMENT AND FEEDBACK FOR LEARNING

Children's awareness of their learning and progress is central to the practice of assessment and feedback for learning (Black and William, 2004). You will become very familiar with the use of assessment and feedback through your training as it is a fundamental part of the planning and teaching process. Assessment for learning (AfL) clearly links to the 'reflective' aspect of Claxton's 4 Rs (Claxton, 2002). AfL provides teachers and children with information so that they know:

○   where they are in their learning, through frequent and timely feedback
    on their learning from their teachers and from each other;

○   where they need to go next, for example, through the sharing of
    learning objectives (eg, 'We are learning to...') and targets;

○   what they need to do in order to reach the next steps in learning: for
    example, through shared success criteria ('What I'm looking for').

Central to AfL is the notion of formative assessment (Clarke, 2005). This is when the information gained about children's learning is used to inform teachers' planning and practice and guide children towards their next steps in learning. The Teachers' Standards (DfE, 2012) state that teachers must *give pupils regular feedback* and *encourage [them] to respond to the feedback*. So through questioning during the introduction to a lesson, a teacher may notice that several children have misunderstood a concept and so will ensure that they are given time to explore this further during the session. Similarly, towards the end of a lesson, children may feed back to the teacher that they have achieved the success criteria and so are ready to work on a further challenge. As with all the approaches discussed in this chapter, assessment for learning is most effective when it is an integral part of classroom practice and is part of the school's ethos.

Teacher voice

Using Assessment for learning

Diane, primary   *This was how we really got started on making a*
head teacher: *difference here and it's the basis of our approach.*
                           Assessment for learning is based on the principle of

> *children being involved in their learning and taking ownership and responsibility for their learning. Children know why they're doing what they're doing. They see what they're doing as part of a bigger picture as teachers will be linking their learning to other activities.*

Reflective task

An awareness of how assessment and feedback are used for learning will help you place learning at the heart of your preparation for teaching.

○   When in school, notice how children are involved in assessment. For example, do they read through each other's work or annotate their own in relation to success criteria?

○   How are children made aware of the purpose of activities and lessons? Perhaps learning objectives are shared with children? Have you seen this done in different ways in different settings? Which do you think was most effective?

BEHAVIOUR FOR LEARNING

Student teachers regularly cite behaviour management as their greatest concern (Chaplain, 2010; Dixie and Bell 2009). Behaviour management consists of techniques and tips that will hopefully enable teachers to stay 'in control' of classes. Additionally, consistent and clear daily routines, rules, rewards and sanctions can play key roles in creating an environment in which learning takes place for all children. Underpinning all of this, however, is the importance of the quality of classroom relationships to children's behaviour. Behaviour for learning (Adams, 2009) is based upon an understanding of the role of relationships in learning. It works on the premise that children's behaviour is affected by three interacting kinds of relationship.

1.   The child's relationship with the curriculum.

2.   The child's relationship with themself.

3.   The child's relationships with others.

The child's relationship with the curriculum

Throughout this chapter, the emphasis has been on children developing a sense of responsibility towards their learning. However, it is the responsibility of adults to provide curricula that reflect the ways in which children learn. For example, play and first-hand and multisensory experiences will encourage engagement and participation, and facilitate learning (Monk and Silman, 2011). The Teachers' Standards reflect this, stating that teachers must use their *knowledge and understanding of how pupils learn and how this impacts on teaching* (DfE, 2012, p 6) as well as use *approaches which are appropriate to pupils' needs in order to involve and motivate them* (DfE, 2012, p 8).

The child's relationship with themself

Children's beliefs and feelings about their ability to learn and how they respond to the challenges and rewards associated with learning play a crucial role in their success at school (Adams, 2009; Higgins et al, 2012). Educationalist John Holt summarises thus: *How much people can learn at any moment depends on how they feel at that moment about the task and their ability to do the task* (Holt, 1984, p 50).

You may have noticed the ways in which some children avoid the challenges that teachers present to them: from prolonged pencil-sharpening to hiding under tables or possibly more vocal and physical behaviours! Adults, therefore, need to help children develop their resilience and ability to manage their emotions. One student teacher, for example, noted that she helped children in her placement class manage their feelings through her acknowledgment and reassurance. *If someone was struggling with something, I'd say, 'it's hard because you're learning, it's the feeling of learning'.* The following examples illustrate the power of making links in learning wherever and whenever it takes place.

Scenario

Developing resilience

Otis in Year 4 was a particularly high achiever in mathematics. However, he lacked enthusiasm for writing and the work he produced was of a poor standard, both in terms of quality and quantity. His teacher knew he was capable of more so he helped Otis to identify the ways in which he approached mathematics and how these could be applied to his writing. For example, Otis enjoyed exploring approaches towards solving mathematical problems before deciding on the best one. So he decided to begin a writing activity by collecting a range of ideas. This gave him several options to draw upon when beginning a piece of written work. It helped Otis to persevere and engage with the writing process. As a result, the quality of his work improved.

Ella in Reception is reflecting on her resilience. She offers an example of her increased resilience when she explains how she's learned to use the monkey bars in the playground near her home. She found this difficult initially but by persevering, she has mastered the skill. Ella identifies that she has displayed resilience as she did not give up and makes links to her developing resilience in the classroom.

The child's relationships with others

This has been explored earlier in this chapter when we looked at learning communities and the relationships nurtured amongst pupils and adults. The Teachers' Standards (DfE, 2012) refer to the necessity for teachers to *maintain good relationships with pupils.* Mutual respect and trust must underpin this. The following example illustrates how children can support each other in promoting their own behaviour for learning.

Scenario

Dealing with distractions

As part of a focus on resourcefulness and resilience, the children within a Year 3 class brainstormed ways in which they could manage distractions. They made a list of examples such as:

○ *say sshhh to the person who's talking;*

○ *fill your mind with what the teacher's saying.*

They decided upon the most useful ideas and these were made into a laminated sign, which was referred to and acted as a reminder. Symbols and images were used in addition to text to illustrate the ideas so that everyone could access the information. Children referred to the sign if someone was distracted. This approach was effective because it was produced by the children and was part of the classroom learning-community ethos.

Reflective task

Consider the views of children from Wales Primary School. They say that successful teachers:

○ *listen to children and are honest;*

○ *make fun trips and exciting lessons;*

○ *let us work in different groups;*

○ *make sure we have the right level of work;*

○ *set challenges;*

○ *have a good personality;*

○ *motivate children.*

○ Try matching each of these characteristics with an aspect of behaviour for learning: relationship with the curriculum; relationship with self; relationship with others (Adams, 2009).

○ The next time you are in a school setting, try to identify the influences on a child's behaviour – which of the three relationships is most relevant?

○ When do you notice children being engaged and enthusiastic?

○ What do you notice are the triggers for unwanted behaviour?

○ Consider your experiences of being at school. What kind of impact did the three relationships of behaviour for learning have on you? Can you identify specific examples?

CONCLUSION

Learning is at the centre of your journey towards becoming a qualified teacher. Your experiences and attitudes in relation to learning will be a major influence on the learning journeys of the children with whom you work. We can't *make* children learn. So developing effective learners is really about respecting and trusting children in their ability to learn as well as being sensitive and responsive to their needs as learners. The approaches we have looked at in this chapter, when implemented effectively, help learners become less dependent on teachers and feel more autonomy and belief in themselves. If you notice examples of these approaches when in school, you will now be able to understand their significance. Your professional curiosity will lead you to consider their impact and this will motivate you to explore ways of creating an environment where learning is enjoyed by everyone.

 Progress checklist

○ Compare attitudes and responses towards learning in Key Stages 1 and 2.

○ Observe children as they are engaged in activities. Keep an open mind and make a note of things that interest you.

○ Notice approaches that help children learn.

○ Consider your own learning and identify how you respond to different experiences and teaching styles. Are you aware of how you respond to learning, eg, what kinds of things spark your curiosity?

○ Nurture your intellectual curiosity; read what takes your interest from the suggested reading lists in this book and this will raise further questions for you to explore.

JARGON BUSTER

Assessment for learning (AfL):	*a term that refers to approaches that develop pupils' awareness and involvement in their learning; for example, teachers use feedback and questioning, and pupils assess their own and each other's work.*
Behaviour for learning:	*an approach aimed at creating a positive classroom climate based upon pupil and teacher relationships and engagement with the curriculum.*
Brain-based learning:	*reflects brain research and aims to make connections between what is currently known about the brain and how best to teach in the light of this.*
First-hand experience:	*visits, visitors and working with historical artefacts are examples of first-hand experiences as these provide children with the opportunity to experience direct interaction (see 'multisensory learning and teaching' below).*
Learning objective:	*a statement that sets out exactly what the teacher intends a child to learn during a lesson or activity.*
Multiple intelligences:	*the idea that we possess a range of intelligences, so teachers need to be aware that their pupils may demonstrate particular strengths and abilities in a range of areas beyond the traditional academic subjects (eg, an ability to work effectively with others), and need to acknowledge and capitalise upon these.*
Multisensory learning and teaching:	*teachers and practitioners enable children to use their senses of sight, hearing, touch (and possibly smell and taste, as appropriate!) through the learning experiences they provide; for example, in a science lesson about plants, children will examine real plants, discussing and dissecting them as well as recording their observations in drawings and diagrams.*
VAK:	*this acronym refers to three styles of learning: visual, auditory and kinaesthetic. The key idea is that most people possess a dominant learning style; in the classroom this may result in teachers*

ensuring they include teaching and learning activities that involve a balance of visual, speaking, listening and musical aids as well as approaches where children are physically active.

 TAKING IT FURTHER

Adams, K (2009) *Behaviour for Learning in the Primary School.* Exeter: Learning Matters.

Useful guide explaining principles and practices associated with behaviour for learning.

Claxton, G (2002) *Building Learning Power.* Bristol: TLO Ltd.

Provides an overview of a strategy for developing effective learners.

Duffy, B (2006) *Supporting Creativity and Imagination in the Early Years.* Maidenhead: Open University Press.

A valuable exploration of young children's learning.

Holt, J (1984) *How Young Children Learn.* London: Penguin.

A classic text – Holt raises fundamental questions about education through insightful observations of individual children.

Pritchard, A (2009) *Ways of Learning: Learning Theories and Learning Styles in the Classroom,* 2nd edition. London: Routledge.

A detailed introduction to theories of learning informing primary education.

REFERENCES

Adams, K (2009) *Behaviour for Learning in the Primary School.* Exeter: Learning Matters.

Black, P and William, D (2004) *Inside the Black Box: Raising Standards through Classroom Assessment.* London: NFER Nelson.

Blakemore, SJ and Frith, U (2005) *The Learning Brain.* Oxford: Blackwell.

Chaplain, R (2010) Managing Classroom Behaviour, in Arthur, J, Grainger, T and Wray, D (eds) *Learning to Teach in the Primary School.* London: Routledge.

Clarke, S (2005). *Formative Assessment in Action: Weaving the Elements Together.* London: Hodder Murray.

Claxton, G (2002) *Building Learning Power.* Bristol: TLO Ltd.

Claxton, G (2005) *The Wayward Mind.* St Ives: Abacus.

Deakin Crick, R (2007) Learning How to Learn: The Dynamic Assessment of Learning Power. *Curriculum Journal,* 18(2): 135–53.

Department for Education (DfE) (2012) *Teachers' Standards.* London: Department for Education. Available at www.webarchive.nationalarchives.gov.uk/20130401151715/ https://www.education.gov.uk/publications/eOrderingDownload/teachers%20 standards.pdf.

Dixie, G (2011) *The Ultimate Teaching Manual: A Route to Success for Beginning Teachers.* London: Continuum.

Dixie, G and Bell, J (2009) *The Trainee Primary Teacher's Handbook.* London: Continuum.

Duffy, B (2006) *Supporting Creativity and Imagination in the Early Years,* 2nd edition. Maidenhead: Open University Press.

Franklin, S (2006) VAKing Out Learning Styles – Why the Notion of 'Learning Styles' is Unhelpful to Teachers. *Education 3–13,* 34(1): 81–7.

Gardner, H (1993) *Frames of Mind: The Theory of Multiple Intelligences,* 10th anniversary edition. New York: Basic Books.

Higgins, S, Kokotsaki, D and Coe, R (2012) *The Teaching and Learning Toolkit.* CEM Centre, Durham University. Available at www.educationendowmentfoundation.org.uk/ library/category/toolkit.

Holt, J (1984) *How Children Learn,* revised edition. London: Penguin.

Howard-Jones, P, Franey, L, Mashmoushi, R and Liao, Y-C (2009) *The Neuroscience Literacy of Trainee Teachers.* Paper presented at the British Educational Research Association Annual Conference, University of Manchester, 2–5 September 2009, University of Bristol, Graduate School of Education. Available at www.70.33.241.170/~neuro647/wp-content/uploads/2012/03/Literacy.pdf.

Illeris, K (ed) (2009) *Contemporary Theories of Learning.* London: Routledge.

Illich, I (1973) *Deschooling Society.* Harmondsworth: Penguin Educational Specials.

Monk, J and Silman, C (2011) *Active Learning in Primary Classrooms.* Harlow: Pearson Education.

Pritchard, A (2009) *Ways of Learning: Learning Theories and Learning Styles in the Classroom,* 2nd edition. London: Routledge.

Sharp, JG, Byrne, J and Bowker, R (2008) VAK or VAK-uous? Towards the Trivialisation of Learning and the Death of Scholarship. *Research Papers in Education,* 23(3): 293–314.

9

Meeting the needs of all learners

Janet Goepel and Naomi Cooper

INTRODUCTION

Children are individuals with differences and similarities and our school populations reflect the diversity we can see in the general population. It is the responsibility of the class teacher to consider the needs of all learners and to embrace the inclusion of all. Inclusion is concerned with all learners; it is about the right for equal recognition, respect and treatment regardless of difference (Armstrong, 2008, p 11). It is tempting to think about children who are 'normal' and identify other children who for one reason or another may appear different. Reasons for difference might include poverty, being of a different race or social class, being from a traveller family or from another country, not speaking English as a first language, having a learning difficulty or a disability, or having a particular physical feature that might contribute towards being considered to be different. This could be as simple as wearing glasses or wearing different clothes from other children. Yet 'normality' depends on the social and geographical environment, the expectations of culture, tradition, the society that we live in and media portrayal. In many instances, it is a shifting concept, with what is different in one situation and at one time becoming 'normal' in another. Take, for example, children born out of marriage. Fifty years ago, to have a baby before marriage was considered to be a matter of great shame and children born to married parents was the norm. However, statistics released by the Office for National Statistics in 2012 show that nearly half of all babies are now born outside of marriage or civil partnership compared with just over 40 per cent in 2002. If this trend continues at the same rate, it will mean that in five years, most children will be born to parents who are not married. This will become the new norm and children born to married parents will be the minority.

In the light of this, it is useful to examine your own idea of what is 'normal' as well as your values and opinions about inclusion and the rights of all learners as this will relate to your expectations of teaching and learning in your classroom if you decide to become a teacher. You will be faced with children who are different and expected to offer them appropriate and meaningful learning opportunities and experiences. While there are many groups of children who you will need to consider, this chapter deals primarily with children with Special Educational Needs or Disabilities (SEND) and those with English as an Additional Language (EAL). However, it is also important to be aware that many of the principles and examples of good practice for children with SEND or EAL are also good practice for all children.

When considering meeting the needs of all learners, it might be tempting to think only of educational needs. However, school environments are places of social value too, where relationships form an important part of the day-to-day experience. You will perhaps think of your own school days in terms of friendships and social contact, and some of the strongest memories you have will be about the people you met and with whom you worked and formed relationships. Children form relationships with their teacher, their peers and a number of other adults in and around school such as midday supervisors, teaching assistants, parent helpers and so on. These relationships contribute to the child's general wellbeing and readiness to learn. Where children are not able to form positive relationships, their ability to learn may be compromised.

Part of being able to form positive relationships are the sense of being accepted and included, and being able to belong and participate within the group. You may have had experiences yourself where you have been part of a group and felt included in their activity. Equally, you may have experienced times when you have felt left out and excluded. Thinking about the different emotions that are evoked by these two experiences may help you to consider what it is like for some of the pupils who may feel excluded from academic or social activity in school.

Research focus

McPhillips, T, Shevlin, M and Long, L (2012) A Right to be Heard: Learning from Learners with Additional Needs in Literacy. *Literacy*, 46(2): 59–66.

McPhillips, Shevlin and Long conducted a small-scale study of the experiences of 9–11-year-old children in the Republic of Ireland and Northern Ireland who were considered by their teachers to need additional support for reading. They explored children's perspectives on support provided and on themselves as readers and writers. The authors describe how the children wanted more information about their teachers' views on their progress in reading and wanted to be given more choices around the kind of support provided. Some also disliked being removed from the classroom for support as they missed out on other activities and disliked the labels others gave them. This research emphasises the importance of gaining children's perspectives on their educational experience.

Reflective task

○   How can we take account of children's perspectives when planning for their learning?

○   How can support be provided in ways that take account of children's emotional, social and learning needs?

The teacher's role in a child's inclusion in school life is not to be underestimated. The way a teacher organises their class, delivers the curriculum and relates to the children in the class all indicate their own stance on inclusion. If a child is continually assigned to a teaching assistant (TA), or taken out of the class, it demonstrates that the teacher has not taken full responsibility for that child and their learning. The intention of supplying TA support and out-of-class learning might be to provide additional support or intervention to support the child's learning needs, but many children find that this identifies them as different and creates a barrier as far as reintegration into class learning is concerned. Additionally, many children who constantly learn separately from their peers, whether in class or out of class, find socialising and friendships more difficult.

Reflective task

Look at the following statements and decide whether you agree or disagree with them.

o   All children should be able to attend their local school regardless of need or disability.

o   Children with learning needs should work with a TA most of the time.

o   Children should work in ability groups for most of the time.

o   The class teacher should change the way they teach and arrange the classroom in order to suit the learning needs of individuals.

o   The class teacher is responsible for the learning needs of all children in their class and cannot allow the demands of one child to detract from the learning experience of the other children.

o   Teachers should not have to manage the disruptive behaviour of some children.

Having considered these statements and your response to them, you will have begun to understand your own values and beliefs a little more. If you consider that all children should be able to attend their local school regardless of need or disability, you are showing a strong inclusive belief that will influence your classroom practice. If you consider however, that children with learning needs should work with a TA most of the time, you may find meeting the needs of all learners a challenge as a teacher.

CONSIDERING ALL LEARNERS

Booth and Ainscow (2002, p 3) describe inclusion as *an unending process of increasing learning and participation for all students ... [Inclusion] happens as soon as the process of increasing participation is started.* They maintain that inclusion recognises the differences between pupils and that inclusive approaches to teaching and learning build on and respect such differences; furthermore, inclusion is concerned with the whole person and is not focused simply on an impairment or the need to learn

EAL. There are many reasons why any child may be excluded. As Booth and Ainscow explore, for example, children with impairments or with EAL may be excluded because the curriculum does not engage their interests or does not acknowledge their home culture.

Some teachers who make regular use of ability groups within their class may place learners with EAL in the lower ability group alongside children with Special Educational Needs (SEN). However, the Special Educational Needs Code of Practice (SENCOP) (DfES, 2001) makes it quite clear that children must not be regarded as having special educational needs simply because English is not their first language, nor the language spoken at home. Children with SEN are one group who are vulnerable to being excluded either from their learning or their peer group, while children with EAL are another.

EQUALITY LEGISLATION AND GUIDANCE

Schools are bound by law in terms of admissions, in order to avoid discrimination. They are also obliged to keep to policy to ensure that they meet the needs of all children regardless of culture, race, language, religion, gender, sexuality, disability or SEN. For example, the Equality Act (2010) requires *reasonable adjustments* to be made where a person with a disability may be disadvantaged in comparison to a person without a disability. Similarly in relation to EAL, the needs of all children are to be considered in order to make planning and delivery of lessons accessible to all.

There are staff members appointed in every school, whose role it is to assist in making their school inclusive. The Special Educational Needs Co-ordinator (SENCO), inclusion manager or EAL lead teacher will have responsibility to support the school team in delivering high quality education for all. Below, read about how one inclusion manager views her responsibilities.

Teacher voice

Including all children

Diane, inclusion manager: *I love my job. It is about making sure all children know that they are important – because they are. Some pupils provide challenges because they find it difficult to learn or difficult to listen or sit still in class but we try to find ways of making sure they reach their potential. This might mean looking at their learning style but it may also mean understanding more about*

> *what makes them tick. A little bit of one-to-one work can really help some children to understand school better and help them see that we as teachers are on their side.*
>
> *Children need to feel safe and secure at school and we want to make sure that they all feel welcome. It is my role to support pupils, parents and teachers so that they are happy with what we do in school. It can be daunting for families and I spend time with them, making sure they understand how we will help their child in school. To be honest, we don't call it inclusion – it is just what we do!*

If you are considering becoming a teacher, then you will need to be mindful of the challenges as well as the joys of making constant adjustments to your practice depending on the nature of the children in your class. As the Children's Act (2004) sets out, every child's wellbeing and inclusion in school are central to their ability to learn.

In the following section, SEND and EAL are examined separately in order to identify critical factors pertaining to each, though you will notice that the underlying principle of inclusion is a constant through both sections.

Special Educational Needs and Disability (SEND)

According to SENCOP, children are considered to have SEN if they *have a learning difficulty which calls for special educational provision to be made for them* (DfES, 2001, p 6). A learning difficulty is defined as having *significantly greater difficulty in learning than the majority of children of the same age*, or having a disability which means they are not able to use the educational facilities provided for children of the same age in their local school (DfES, 2001, p 6). Recent figures released by the government (DfE, 2012) show that nearly 22 per cent of boys at primary age are considered to have SEN while for girls the figure is 12 per cent. This means that when you are working in schools, you are much more likely to encounter boys with SEN than girls, as the examples of children's voices in this chapter show.

Currently, revisions to legislation, policy and guidance are taking place. One of the most recently introduced documents is the Green Paper *Support and Aspiration: A New Approach to Special Educational Needs and Disability* (DfE, 2011) to be made legal through the Children and Families Bill (2013). Fundamental to this Bill is the introduction of a single early years setting and school-based category of SEN with the intention of early identification of need. Additionally, a single Education, Health and Care Plan (EHCP), which some children with more significant educational needs may have, will be introduced with the intention that health, education and social services will work together more closely to meet the needs of other such children.

Removing barriers to learning: SEN

The 2004 government publication *Removing Barriers to Achievement* states: *Inclusion is about much more than the type of school that children attend; it is about the quality of their experience; how they are helped to learn, achieve and participate fully in the life of the school* (DfES, 2004, p 35). This puts the onus on the teacher to recognise barriers to learning in their classroom and be willing to make changes which will provide smoother access to learning for all.

The new draft national curriculum in England also sets out inclusive principles. They are:

○ setting suitable challenges;

○ responding to pupils' needs and overcoming potential barriers for individuals and groups of pupils (DfE, 2013, p 9).

The new national curriculum also reminds the teacher of their duties within the Equality Act (2010) and of their responsibility to plan lessons so that *there are no barriers to every child achieving* (DfE, 2013, p 9). Included in the inclusion statements is specific reference to children with SEND and also children with EAL. In each case the teacher is charged with the responsibility of ensuring that all children can access appropriate learning.

Models of disability

There are two predominant models of disability, the medical model and the social model. The medical model looks at the person as having a deficit or condition that does not allow them to function as other people might. It is considered that this deficit should be fixed and the person 'normalised' through diagnosis, treatment, intervention and where possible cure (Farrell, 2004, p 68). SENCOP is based on identifying a child's need, early intervention and making *adequate progress* (DfES, 2001, p 52) and in this way could be considered to be operating within the medical model.

Underpinning the ideals in the Equality Act (2010) is the social model of disability. The social model of disability considers that barriers to learning and participation occur because of a disabling environment – in this model people are usually referred to as being 'disabled' by these environmental factors, rather than as 'having disabilities'. This might be related to concerns of access such as ramps and lifts, but could also be related to access to the academic and social aspects of school life such as curriculum activities, after-school clubs and break-times. This does not mean that a child's impairment is ignored, but rather that attitudes, physical barriers, organisation, structures and prac-tices are challenged such that learning and participation can take place and alongside peers (Booth and Ainscow, 2002, p 7). Similarly, Booth and Ainscow make the point that inclusion is not just for those with obvious impairments or learning needs, but is about *minimising* all *barriers in education for* all *students* (Booth and Ainscow, 2002, p 3).

The Office for Disability Issues identifies the barriers that create disability as:

○ the environment – including inaccessible buildings and services;

○ people's attitudes – stereotyping, discrimination and prejudice;

○ organisations – inflexible policies, practices and procedures.

The following website offers further information about the social model and ways to understand disability: www.odi.dwp.gov.uk/about-the-odi/the-social-model.php.

Micheline Mason and Jonathan Bartley took part in a BBC debate about including children with disabilities in mainstream schools. This can be found at www.michelinemason.com/inclusive-education.

Reflective task

After visiting the above website and watching the debate, consider:

○ whether you think special schools lead to discrimination;

○ whether segregated schools lead to a segregated society;

○ the significance of the inclusion of disabled pupils for the culture of a school;

○ how you feel about being the teacher of children with disabilities.

LABELLING CHILDREN

Barriers to learning may take many forms, and the way teachers identify and refer to children with SEND can be problematic for the learner. Children are no longer referred to as 'handicapped', 'spastic', 'morons' or 'cretins', as these have become terms of abuse, yet these were all once medical terms used to describe children with various medical conditions. The term 'Special Educational Needs' is now commonly used but this too is in danger of falling into disrepute. Being 'special' may not now be seen as a term of endearment, but of being needy and different.

Teacher voice

The effect of labelling children

Michael: *In my experience as a teacher and SENCO, parents were often resistant to their children being identified as having SEN, as they disliked the stigma they felt was attached to this label. Marking a child out as having SEN identified them as 'different', often requiring out-of-class interventions and reducing their opportunities to work alongside their classmates. This in turn* *contributed to increased social isolation, which brought about a sense of not belonging and loss of confidence, resulting in a compromised disposition for learning. Labelling children therefore can be seen as creating a barrier to learning. However, identifying a child's needs can ensure that these needs are recognised and catered for in an appropriate manner.*

Scenario

Labelling and barriers to learning

Bradley is nine years old. He attends a mainstream junior school. He has a diagnosis of Attention Deficit Hyperactivity Disorder (ADHD). Bradley often calls out in class and so his teacher considers he is attention-seeking. He has a special cushion to sit on that enables him to take his concentration from trying to sit still to engaging with his work. He frequently gets up and walks around the classroom and fiddles with things on other children's desks causing the teacher to think he is lazy and probably not very academically able. Bradley has a stress ball to grasp to enable him to fiddle with things on his own desk. His writing is poor and he finds it difficult to orientate himself to be able to look at the board and copy things from it. The teacher wonders whether this is an excuse and thinks he needs to try harder with his work. The ADHD nurse has recommended that Bradley should sit at the front of the class facing the board so as to make things easier for him. However, the class teacher has moved him to sit at the back of the class, alone and facing a side wall. She states that she has put him in that position so he is out of sight of the other children as he distracts them. She thinks that he enjoys the tendency to be the 'class clown'. However, in this position, his writing and work output reduces further as he is unable to access the work on the board as he has to turn sideways to see it.

Reflective task

o   What labels has the class teacher given Bradley?

o   How might these labels indicate what the class teacher thinks of Bradley?

o   What barriers to the curriculum is Bradley experiencing and how might they be reduced or removed?

- ○ What environmental barriers is Bradley experiencing and how might they be reduced or removed?

- ○ How do you think Bradley perceives himself within the class and what can the class teacher do to improve his image?

Children with SEN often find it distressing and frustrating to be considered to have a deficit and for 'normalisation' to be expected. Their parents often find this distressing and frustrating too. Consider the perspectives of Joshua and his mother as given below. Joshua does not have an identified SEN despite being assessed for dyspraxia. However, some of his teachers have complained that he gets into trouble when standing in a line, that he fiddles with things and falls off his chair.

Scenario

Joshua's story

Joshua, aged ten: *When I get things wrong it makes me feel stupid. I don't think I'm being naughty, but doing what I thought I should be doing and then I think oops, I'm not doing the right thing. Once when I did some writing I made sure the content of my work was good because that was one of my targets. The teacher, who was the cover teacher, looked at my handwriting and saw it wasn't as good as some of my other handwriting, so she tore the work out of the book. She said it wasn't my best work, but I had been working on content not handwriting. She made me stay behind when the rest of the class went into the hall to use the new climbing wall. I was disappointed and upset. The teacher told me that when I had finished my work I could put my book on her desk and go and join the class in the hall. When I did, I got told off for not asking permission from the teaching assistant, but I had done exactly what I had been told to do.*

Joshua's mum: *Our experience of school has been mixed. At times Joshua has been expected to accommodate to the expectations of others rather than his needs being understood and met by the professionals, for* *example as a four- and five-year-old he was labelled as naughty because he couldn't sit or stand still and was clumsy. The 'solution' was to make him sit on a small square of carpet at the back when the children had carpet time. He felt like he let his class down when lining up in the yard because there were rewards for the 'neatest' line. These things may be small, but they felt exclusive and unkind. As a parent of a 'compliant' child, it was difficult to see him try and fail to achieve the standards set by the teachers and be labelled as naughty, yet know he could not achieve what was being asked of him. As a consequence he developed poor self-esteem. I am glad to say that he has also had some very positive, understanding teachers who have worked hard to be inclusive and rebuild his confidence.*

Reflective task

Thinking about Joshua's experience in the scenario above:

o   What is your reaction to how the cover teacher responded to Joshua?

o   What could she have done differently?

o   How could the self-esteem of a child like Joshua be preserved?

Thinking about Joshua's mum's comments:

o   What do you think about her observation that *at times Joshua has been expected to accommodate to the expectations of others rather than his needs being understood and met by the professionals*?

o   How important do you think school expectations such as having a 'neat line' are and what are the consequences of this for children such as Joshua?

o   What role do you think parents such as Joshua's mum have in helping the class teacher to understand children who learn differently or have different abilities with regard to behaviour?

The following are one student teacher's comments about what he learned while working with Billy, who is diagnosed as having Down's Syndrome. At the time he was working with a group of children who all struggled with the subject. This student teacher's approach is markedly different from that of the cover teacher who Joshua talks about.

Student teacher voice

Learning from practice

Daniel, student teacher: *Through this experience [working with Billy] I learned that placing the needs, capabilities and inclusion of Billy at the very centre of my teaching was one of the most effective things that I did to make my classroom inclusive for all. While I think that this would have been more of a challenge had I taught a class with a far wider range of abilities ... I nevertheless understood the extent to which including the child with the most complex needs, the most potentially excluded child, is important not just for the child in question, but for the social and educational inclusivity of a classroom that values each and every child within it.*

ENGLISH AS AN ADDITIONAL LANGUAGE

The National Association for Language Development in the Curriculum (NALDIC) defines EAL as the *term used to describe the learning of English in addition to the learner's first language. The term EAL recognises that, for some learners, English may be their third or fourth language* (NALDIC, 2013).

EAL is not the same as SEN. Of course, sometimes, learners may have additional learning needs related to SEN but this should never be assumed. EAL learners may be gifted in any curriculum area – they just cannot yet communicate this in English. EAL is a growing priority in schools as we have many children arriving into the United Kingdom on a regular basis. Our fastest growing group of new arrivals is currently from Eastern Europe, though some schools cater for children from a vast array of countries.

Teacher voice

Working with EAL learners

Pauline, teacher: *Our school is in an area of the city where many newly arrived asylum seekers first come to stay. Often families* *do not stay for long in the community before moving on to more permanent accommodation. This means that children are often not with us in school for more than a few weeks or months. I teach children whose first language is one (or more) of the following: Albanian/Shqip, Amharic, Arabic, Bengali, Bengali (Sylheti), Chinese, Dutch/Flemish, English, Hindi, Kurdish, Panjabi, Pashto/Pakhto, Persian/Farsi, Polish, Russian, Somali, Spanish, Swahili/Kiswahili, Tamil, Urdu.*

Teaching can be challenging when there are many children whose first language is not English. Even if there is only one child in the school for whom English is an additional language, teachers still need to make provision for that child's learning.

While EAL is not synonymous with matters of race, culture, heritage and religion, there will sometimes be overlapping factors. No two children are the same, as the following scenario highlights:

Scenario

Recognising difference

Jamaal joined primary school in Year 3 (7–8 years old). He had recently moved from Somalia with his family, following a period of political unrest. Jamaal had witnessed troubling events in his home town and had lost a member of his close family there. He joined school at the same time as his older brother Abshir. They were both silent for about two weeks but after this time, Abshir quickly began to settle into school life and grasped early English easily. Jamaal did not socialise with others at break time or show any signs of beginning to join in with class lessons. He spent as much time as possible with his brother. Jamaal remained a very quiet member of the class for the whole school year, often giving the appearance of being bewildered by the demands of school life. Abshir went on to achieve well academically and socially.

> ## *Reflective task*
>
> ○ What factors did the class teachers need to know about in order to teach Jamaal and Abshir effectively?
>
> ○ How could the whole school support Jamaal socially?
>
> ○ Why were Jamaal and Abshir different from each other? Why didn't they both settle into school in the same way?
>
> ○ Is an understanding of Jamaal and Abshir's background important? If so, why?

Language acquisition

Cummins (1984) suggests that the language that children hear and begin to use in school may be placed on a continuum between 'everyday communicative language' – such as words and phrases used in the playground and other social situations – to more abstract 'academic language', such as that used in a lesson on, for example, photosynthesis. Cummins' research demonstrated that children acquired basic communicative language very quickly and often became fluent within two years. He found that the academic language, which is habitually learned in a more abstract, intellectual way, was not fully embedded until the child had been learning English for five to seven years. This has implications for the class teacher. Teachers must plan with the needs of all pupils in mind and, of course, not all pupils are the same.

Teaching children with EAL can be a highly stimulating experience that helps children build on what they already know. Gravelle (2000) suggests that teachers should be noting and enquiring as to what EAL learners bring to the classroom community and to the task of learning. Gravelle highlights, for example, that pupils' social skills are important as well as their linguistic and cognitive skills. Once the teacher understands such factors, they can plan the teaching and support necessary to optimise learning.

Student teacher voice

Teaching strategies in practice

Lisa, student teacher: *I was in a school where 99 per cent of children were EAL learners, working in Year 5 (with 9–10-year-old children). Their needs ranged from 'new to English' to full competence in speaking, listening, reading and writing. The fact that children are new to English affects all of their learning. I had children* *who were working on P levels because they had SEN as well as EAL all through to learners who were working at a very high level. I used visual aids all of the time. I used a visual timetable and they loved it. As often as I could, I used multisensory learning in all subjects – especially in maths and foundation subjects. Children with EAL were often amazing in PE [physical education] because they could watch others and quickly knew what to do. PE was a lesson where EAL children could really shine from the start. In literacy, the lower group was often withdrawn from class so that they could go and work with an EAL support teacher. I used AfL [Assessment for learning; see Chapter 8] all the time, I repeated everything. I usually worked with the middle ability group (when the lower ability group was withdrawn) as they needed more reinforcement because of EAL.*

There are a number of misconceptions about language learning that it is important to avoid. For example, research (McLaughlin, 1992) shows that young children do not necessarily learn languages faster than adults; they do not necessarily feel more confident in taking risks and making mistakes; they do not learn a new language more quickly as a result of being immersed in it to the exclusion of their home language. Indeed, we know that it is very important for children to continue to use their home language alongside learning another one. This is partly because children will switch from one language to another or move seamlessly between the two in order to aid understanding. It is also because the underlying skills of language learning, which are more advanced in the first language, support the learning of second or subsequent languages (Cummins, 2000). Often, children's language development will be aided if they are allowed to use and communicate in both the new language and their home language(s). These factors are important to remember – children will only learn a new language given sufficient time, opportunities and appropriate support from the teacher.

Scenario

Language development

Angelica joined school in Year 2 (aged seven years). As a new arrival, she knew and understood little English. Angelica's spoken English developed quickly. After approximately 18 months, a visitor to the class could not tell that Angelica's first language was not English. However, her written work took three more years to meet the same standard as others who were a similar 'profile' on non-verbal reasoning scores from tests administered in Year 3.

Reflective task

○ If you have experience of learning a second/additional language – for example as a student at school or by travelling abroad:

- How did you feel when faced with a language you did not understand?

- What were the words and phrases you learned first?

- What/who did you find helped most? Was it someone who could speak the language which you were learning – and perhaps your home language too?

○ Consider the pros and cons of using home language in a school context.

○ How might teachers support pupils with EAL?

SEN AND EAL: MAKING LEARNING ACCESSIBLE

Children can be placed in the classroom in a way that disadvantages their learning. Thinking about your own schooling, you would probably have a preferred place to sit within the classroom and liked to choose the people you worked with. This may have been based on friendships and hopefully was effective as far as learning was concerned. Children with SEND may need specific provision in order for them to be able to access opportunities to learn. This may include being seated so they can see the whiteboard clearly, having clear access if a wheelchair is required or having an individual work station if the noise and stimulus of other children hinders learning. Similarly children may benefit from having coloured overlays to support reading, specific writing implements or sloping desks to support writing, or specialist cushions or chairs to support posture. Other learning difficulties require the teacher to know the child and to provide particular approaches to support their learning.

Adult voice

Teacher expectations

Mark is an adult with a significant stammer. When he was a child in school, his teachers thought he was hard working. On his school report, his effort grades were always very high. Here are his perceptions of his disability and his definitions of a good teacher.

Mark: *I didn't see my stammer as part of me. It controlled me and did things to me I hated. I imagined who I would be if I didn't have the stammer. I tried hard with my writing, because speaking was so difficult in class. The worst thing in school was sitting in a circle, with each child expected to say something. I had a sense of absolute dread. If I say something without thinking, I am fluent. If I'm asked a question and there is only one answer, I can't say it.*

For me, the good teachers were the ones who gave me time to speak and didn't guess what I was trying to say. Good teachers tried not to look frustrated or embarrassed as this put me under pressure. Good teachers asked what could be done to help – many just assumed they knew.

If there is a TA available to work with a class, it is important for the class teacher to communicate clear expectations to the TA about how they should work with different groups of children. It can be very challenging to find the time and opportunity in a busy school day to liaise with a TA or indeed other adult helpers. However, in order to bring about effective learning for children with additional needs such as SEN or EAL, the teacher needs to work closely with additional adults as well as group the children in her class carefully and plan challenging but realistic learning tasks (see Chapter 2).

As a teacher, you will be expected to teach children with SEND. Here is the experience of one teacher who found she had a child with significant learning difficulties in her first class as a newly qualified teacher. The child needed oxygen to support her breathing and her only means of communication was through eye movement.

Newly qualified teacher voice

Voicing complexity

When I was offered the job I was told about Elizabeth (not her real name). I think I was a bit naïve really. She can't access anything on her own. I share all my planning with Elizabeth's support worker. When we have carpet time, Elizabeth

> *joins in by having her wheelchair positioned appropriately. Sometimes the environment is a challenge, we have to shuffle things round and sometimes we have to take things to Elizabeth. When it is one-to-one reading, she can say yes or no by her eyes and she changes her gaze to find particular characters. Sometimes I think am I doing enough for her, but I have 29 other children too, but it's the little things that you do. The other children in the class are very accepting. It has been wonderful for them. I would say that having a child like Elizabeth in the classroom shouldn't put any one off. It gives you a more rounded view of being a teacher.*

Teaching children who are learning EAL can be a challenging area of primary school teaching too. It can also be highly rewarding. Presenting yourself as a learner, as well as a class teacher, may be a helpful role model for children in your class. Children will gain confidence from the reassurance that all of us are learners all of the time. They will feel valued if you model that they are welcome in your class and the fact that they do not (yet) speak much English is not a problem. If you commit to learning one or two phrases in the child's home language (where this is feasible) this will help children to feel that their home language is important to you. We know that children learn more effectively when they feel relaxed and safe. Growth in pupils' self-esteem (Siraj-Blatchford et al, 2008) as a consequence of the teacher's willing acceptance will become a good foundation for children's learning.

Teaching that specifically plans to support EAL learners will also provide structure and support for other members of your class. For example, using a 'visual timetable' supports EAL learners but will also support pupils who feel more secure from knowing what the structure of their day will be. Similarly, banks of vocabulary with accompanying pictures, compiled to support learning in a literacy lesson, will support *all* learners.

We need to be flexible in our teaching, depending on who is in our class and the additional adults who are assisting (if any). Some children will benefit from having parts of each lesson repeated or revisited in order to reinforce learning, and all EAL learners as well as children with SEN will need to be given opportunities to talk extensively about new knowledge, vocabulary and understanding. Both EAL learners and those with SEN will benefit from a range of visual prompts and support for their language needs. All opportunities to support learners visually should be utilised to the full – pictures, vocabulary lists, writing grids, actions and gestures are all part of teaching learners with different needs. Sometimes there is a need to work on a one-to-one basis with children either in class or withdrawn from whole-class teaching for a short time. As one trainee teacher who had just completed a block placement in a school which a high proportion of EAL learners said: *I was scared before I went into school but soon realised that it was like any other. I really enjoyed getting to know the children* (Jade, final year student teacher).

Teacher voice

Challenges or opportunities?

Teaching in a school that has a high mobility of pupils and large percentage of pupils with EAL (and for whom this presents a barrier to their learning either for part or the whole of the time they are with us) presents teachers at our school with circumstances that will not be present in all other schools. It could be described as a 'challenge' to deliver the curriculum effectively to all the children in our care and indeed it is, but actually, we prefer to use the term 'opportunity'. We, as teachers of these children, are charged with the responsibility of bringing the curriculum to life for all our children. Finding ways to do this sparks our creativity and enthusiasm for the job. Nothing beats witnessing that 'light bulb' moment when a child's face lights up with the pure pleasure of understanding, and you know you have played a key part in that process.

The needs of our EAL learners are met because we ensure our planning is tailored to the next step targets of all our children and in doing so, consider how we enable all to access the curriculum. A key factor to achieving this is our ability to make abstract concepts 'tangible' through the provision of concrete experiences as much as possible, for as long as is required, throughout the primary years. These are actually the key elements of sound primary teaching anyway.

CONCLUSION

We hope that by reading this chapter, you will have gained an insight into the many and varied challenges of working with a range of learners in a primary classroom. In every class of children, there will be those who present specific needs of one kind or another. However, all children are unique and come to school with their own particular set of circumstances. It is important that, if you are hoping to enter the teaching profession, you are interested in *people* as well as being interested in *education*. As teachers we engage on a professional level with many different people – pupils, parents, other teachers, additional adults such as teaching assistants, and professionals from other areas such as health and social care. This engagement is governed in some way by our personal commitment to meeting the needs of all learners in our care.

Progress checklist

○ When you visit school, spend some time with a child who has a barrier to learning. Gain a holistic perspective of this child.

○ Listen to different children's stories about their lives. Talk to the SENCO in a school about strategies they suggest to class teachers to support the inclusion of all pupils.

○ Observe how teaching assistants are used to support children with SEN or EAL. What does this tell you about the inclusive practice in the school?

○ Identify inclusive strategies during your visits to school. Use some of the ideas outlined in this chapter to help you.

○ Keep a diary about your days in school. As you understand children who you are working with more fully, how do your feelings towards inclusion change? Or does your experience in school confirm what you already thought/ believed before you began?

JARGON BUSTER

Language acquisition: *the process by which pupils learn language in spoken or written form.*

Multisensory learning: *using more than one sense in the learning task – eg, tracing letter shapes in the sand with your finger as well as looking at them on a page.*

NVR: *Non-Verbal Reasoning tests are used to determine pupils' abilities independent of language skills.*

P levels: *assessment measures use to assess those with SEN who have not yet met Level 1 national curriculum criteria.*

Special Educational Code of Practice (SENCOP): *provides a framework for schools for supporting children with SEN. Available at www.webarchive.nationalarchives.gov. uk/20130401151715/https://www.education. gov.uk/publications/eOrderingDownload/ DfES%200581%20200mig2228.pdf.*

Special Educational Needs Co-ordinator (SENCO):	teacher in school responsible for ensuring that effective support for children with SEN is provided.
Visual timetable*:*	a timetable showing each lesson of the day in picture format so that children know which lessons will be happening that day and in which order. This may be displayed on the classroom wall or other accessible place in the classroom.

 TAKING IT FURTHER

Conteh, J (2012) *Teaching Bilingual and EAL Learners in Primary Schools.* London: Sage.

Practical guidance for working with children with EAL.

Department for Education and Skills (DfES) (2004) *Removing Barriers to Achievement: The Government's Strategy for SEN.* Nottingham: DfES Publications. Available at www.education.gov.uk/lamb/resources/ Universal/removing_barriers.pdf.

This is the previous government's strategy for SEN in England. It provides an excellent insight into previous policy and an important understanding of how children with SEN can be supported to achieve.

Mason, M (2000) *Incurably Human.* London: Working Press.

Traces the life of Micheline Mason, who is disabled. She outlines how her disability is perceived by others, describes her upbringing and shows how her strong belief in equality has impacted on her life and how she has become an advocate for other disabled people.

McLaughlin, B (1992) *Education Practice Report 5: Myths and Misconceptions about Second Language Learning: What Every Teacher Needs to Unlearn.* University of California, Santa Cruz: National Center for Research on Cultural Diversity and Second Language Learning.

Explores commonly held beliefs about how children learn additional languages and clarifies misconceptions.

Richards, G and Armstrong, F (eds) (2010) *Teaching and Learning in Inclusive and Diverse Classrooms.* London: Routledge.

Outlines a wide variety of issues concerned with inclusion and diversity. Topics include: ethnic diversity, gender, traveller children, challenging behaviour, bullying and SEN.

www.naldic.org.uk

National Association for Language Development in the Curriculum. An excellent website including many links to academic articles, teaching resources and stories which help to illustrate the needs of EAL learners.

www.youtube.com/watch?v=ekj2dmGLMNo

A Disability Awareness video exploring the Disability Discrimination Act and what this means in practice. It considers the medical and social models of disability and classroom approaches.

REFERENCES

Armstrong, F (2008) Inclusive Education, in Richards, G and Armstrong, F (eds) *Key Issues for Teaching Assistants: Working in Diverse and Inclusive Classrooms*. London: Routledge.

Booth, T and Ainscow, M (2002) *The Index for Inclusion: Developing Learning and Participation in Schools*. Bristol: Centre for Studies on Inclusive Education.

Cummins, J (1984) *Bilingualism and Special Education*. Clevedon: Multilingual Matters.

Cummins, J (2000) *Language, Power and Pedagogy: Bilingual Children in the Crossfire*. Clevedon: Multilingual Matters.

Department for Education (DfE) (2011) *Support and Aspiration: A New Approach to Special Educational Needs and Disability*. London: The Stationery Office. Available at www.webarchive.nationalarchives.gov.uk/20130401151715/https://www.education. gov.uk/publications/eOrderingDownload/Green-Paper-SEN.pdf.

Department for Education (DfE) (2012) *Children with Special Educational Needs: An Analysis – 2012*. London: Crown Publications. Available at www.gov.uk/government/ uploads/system/uploads/attachment_data/file/219510/sfr24-2012c1.pdf.

Department for Education (DfE) (2013) *The National Curriculum in England: Framework Document for Consultation*. London: Crown Publications. Available at www.media. education.gov.uk/assets/files/pdf/n/national%20curriculum%20consultation%20 -%20framework%20document.pdf.

Department for Education and Skills (DfES) (2001) *Special Educational Needs Code of Practice*. Nottingham: DfES Publications, HMSO. Available at www.webarchive. nationalarchives.gov.uk/20130401151715/https://www.education.gov.uk/ publications/eOrderingDownload/DfES%200581%20200mig2228.pdf.

Department for Education and Skills (DfES) (2004) *Removing Barriers to Achievement: The Government's Strategy for SEN*. Nottingham: DfES Publications. Available at www.education.gov.uk/lamb/resources/Universal/removing_barriers.pdf.

Farrell, M (2004) *Special Educational Needs: A Resource for Practitioners*. London: Paul Chapman Publishing.

Gravelle, M (2000) *Planning for Bilingual Learners*. Stoke on Trent: Trentham.

McLaughlin, B (1992) *Education Practice Report 5: Myths and Misconceptions about Second Language Learning: What Every Teacher Needs to Unlearn*. University of California, Santa Cruz: National Center for Research on Cultural Diversity and Second Language Learning.

National Association for Language Development in the Curriculum (NALDIC) (2013) *EAL Glossary*. Available at www.naldic.org.uk/eal-teaching-and-learning/eal-glossary.

Office for National Statistics (2012) *Births in England and Wales 2012*. Available at www.ons.gov.uk/ons/dcp171778_317196.pdf.

Siraj-Blatchford, I, Clarke, K and Needham, M (eds) (2008) *The Team Around the Child: Multi-Agency Working in the Early Years*. London: Trentham Books.

10 Conclusion
David Owen

This chapter summarises the key themes discussed in the book and outlines how preparing to become a primary teacher may change in the future. It reviews the current employment prospects for those in training and also considers how they might enhance their employment prospects after gaining a place on a teacher preparation programme.

KEY THEMES

Key themes identified in this book include developing your self-awareness as a teacher, applying subject knowledge to learning and listening to children. Chapters 2, 3 and 4 focused on reflection, identity and experience; these chapters all involved identifying your personal potential to flourish in a primary school work environment. Chapter 2 showed how important it is to consider the personal motivations, feelings and emotions bound up in the life of a teacher. In Chapter 3 we saw the benefits of immersing yourself in your pre-application experience in order to ensure that (or establish whether) teaching is likely to be the right profession for you, and indeed that (or whether) you are right for the profession. Chapter 4 provided an overview of the reflective journey you need to make during your initial teacher preparation programme.

Chapters 5 and 6 introduced a deeper level of development: it is not enough just to have experience and be self-aware; you need to develop a critical view on the curriculum, the nature of subject knowledge and what you are asked to teach in schools. Curriculum guidance and government policy change rapidly. Schools have more autonomy in some ways than ever before so you need to develop strategies to assess policy and develop your knowledge and skills using critical thinking and enquiry-based learning.

Chapters 7, 8, and 9 took you beyond the basics to really focus not on you and your teaching, but on the pupils and their learning. The value of creativity and tirelessly searching for imaginative ways to engage children in learning cannot be underestimated. Chapter 7 explored the freedom that schools now have to create their own individual teaching schemes and the challenge of being creative and engaging the children and the wider community. Chapter 8 stressed the recent work in schools that focuses on children's awareness of the process of learning and developing a spirit of enquiry. Throughout the book the authors have featured the 'voices' of pupils and their teachers. Chapter 9 stressed the importance of really listening to pupils' voices and continually striving towards inclusion.

The authors hope that the developments addressed throughout the book have stimulated your thoughts about primary teaching and presented you with the tools to put together a successful application and interview for any current initial teacher preparation programmes. The next section briefly considers possible future developments and changes that may be useful to know about when developing your application.

FUTURE CHANGES

School-led teacher education has been in the ascendance since 2011 in England. The current government's policy is to create the conditions for schools to be more autonomous in how they recruit and train teachers. This may mean that recruitment into teaching is not distributed evenly across different regions in the next few years, or that there may be too many teachers trained in one area and too few in another part of the country. However it is hard to predict what will happen given that many schools are applying to work as School Direct partners, but may only apply for small numbers of training places.

Increasing numbers of primary schools are now part of academy chains, teaching school alliances or federations of schools working together. This creates the conditions for groups of schools to recruit teachers to a 'pool' for an alliance or academy chain. It may be that schools will increasingly group together to recruit across a particular region (for example the Schools Partnership Trust have a network of more than 40 schools across the north of England and recruit to the overall organisation rather than to specific schools).

This book has focused specifically on becoming a primary teacher in England as currently the Department for Education specifies that teachers need Qualified Teacher Status to work in most English state-funded schools. However, currently you do not need to be a qualified teacher to work in a free school. What if this was extended more widely to academies or all state primary schools? It would then be more possible to undertake your preparation in a school in another country in the European Union. Recruitment from Australia and Canada has been an important part of teacher supply for many years, for example. The impact of the cost of tuition fees for degree and PGCE courses could push some would-be teachers to study abroad and then return to teach in England. Already there are examples of students completing their undergraduate degrees in England then studying for a Master's degree in Education in international schools as part of an international teaching qualification.

It is also worth imagining what might be the likely impact of continued improvements in digital communications and computing. At what point may it be an option for aspects of individualised primary education to take place at home via the internet? The rationale for grouping children into classes of 20–30 and physically locating them in a school may become weaker as more and more parents and carers work from home. It may be that primary school becomes a place to learn face-to-face interaction and social skills if other aspects of the curriculum can be taught via digital media.

EMPLOYMENT PROSPECTS

The employment prospects for prospective primary teachers in England are good. Numbers in nursery and primary schools started rising in 2010 and are projected to increase until at least 2020. Predictions made in 2012 suggested there would be an 18 per cent increase over this period to a figure of 4,826,000 pupils learning in primary schools across England in 2020 (DfE, 2012).

These demographic statistics will mean there will be a constant demand for more primary teachers. The impact of pupil premium funding is also likely to lead to an increased demand for full- and part-time primary teachers. Pupil premium funding is provided to each state primary school for children in receipt of free school meals, 'looked after' children and children from Armed Forces families. In 2013 this was £900 per year for each child in either of these categories. This funding has been used in many cases to employ more teachers to teach children before and after school, and during the school holidays.

Enhancing your chances of getting a job

Even though the present day chances of getting a job are high, you can enhance these chances by applying many of the ideas discussed in this book. Peter Hooper, the head teacher featured in Chapter 3, gave the following advice to new teachers:

I need somebody who has the confidence to hit the ground running, to make mistakes and to learn from them quickly. I need individuals who can make an impact and whose individuality can quickly contribute to the bigger picture. When interviewing, and perhaps more importantly when shortlisting, I need to see something of the individual shine through. Too many applications are bland and uninteresting and consequently fall at the first hurdle. I want to appoint enthusiastic and vibrant teachers who can show that they can motivate and inspire. I expect to have to support them but I want to be reining them in rather than dragging them forward.

Just as you need to present your individuality to be successful when applying for an initial teacher preparation programme, so you need to show your individuality when applying for a teaching post as a newly qualified teacher (NQT). You need to give examples of the impact you will have on the children you teach, and to demonstrate how you will develop into an outstanding teacher.

CONTINUING PROFESSIONAL DEVELOPMENT

As Jane Bartholomew argues in Chapter 8, successful teachers demonstrate they are learners too. Initial teacher preparation is followed by a range of opportunities for continuing professional development (CPD). These opportunities can take many forms, from twilight or early morning staff meetings to embarking on a Masters degree, education doctorate or PhD. If you completed a PGCE or four-year undergraduate course you are likely to have already started your Masters study so will be able to continue this.

As an NQT you will need to further develop your skills and consider whether you want to specialise in an area of the curriculum, perhaps by first shadowing a subject co-ordinator in her/his work. Or perhaps you are interested in supporting others who want to enter the profession? Working with an experienced mentor or school-based tutor and considering how you might in the future guide new entrants to the profession may be an appropriate goal.

During your NQT period your teaching will continue to be observed and you will continue to work with a mentor. You are also likely to continue to have to write lesson plans and to evaluate your work for formal observations. If you are serious about developing into an excellent teacher of primary school children, you should try to see all of this not as a hassle or an inconvenience, as some do, but rather as an opportunity to be grasped with both hands. Make full use of your mentor while you still have one, and never stop being a critically reflective practitioner!

REFERENCES

Department for Education (DfE) (2012). National Pupil Projections: Future Trends in Pupil Numbers – July 2012. Available at www.gov.uk/government/uploads/system/uploads/attachment_data/file/219536/osr152012.pdf.

Index